Jacques Tissot:
139 Masterpieces

By Maria Tsaneva

First Edition

I0477164

*****

Jacques Tissot: 140 Paintings and Drawings
*****

Foreword

Jacques-Joseph Tissot was born in 1836, in Nantes in a seaport on the French coast. Throughout his life Tissot retained an affinity and fascination with all things naval, and his marked ability to accurately paint rigging and shipboard scene paintings must have come from his boyhood. Tissot was the son of a very prosperous, successful shopkeeper, who was a devout Roman Catholic. Unsurprisingly the young Tissot was sent away to a boarding school run by Jesuits. Tissot senior seems to have been unenthusiastic about the prospect of his son becoming an artist, but eventually accepted the inevitability of his son's artistic pretensions forming the basis of his career.

In 1856 Tissot went to Paris to train as a painter. Here, at the Ecole des Beaux Arts the young Tissot met the young James McNiell Whistler (1834-1903), one of the most celebrated and unusual figures in 19th century art. At about this time Tissot also met, and became a friend of Degas (1834-1917) the Impressionist painter. Like Alma-Tadema, and Edward Burne-Jones, Tissot changed his name at this time to draw attention to himself. In his case he anglicised his Christian name to James. Tissot had fully inherited the sharp commercial instincts of his father, and again like Alma-Tadema and Millais was a painter-entrepreneur. In the 1860s the painter became something of a traveller, visiting Italy, and in 1862 London. In 1864 Tissot exhibited his oil paintings at the Royal Academy for the first time, suggesting that he realised the potential of London as a source of wealthy patrons. Tissot began to concentrate on contemporary scene paintings at this time. In 1869 he produced caricatures for Vanity Fair magazine, where "Spy" had been the celebrated producer of this type of work for many years. Tissot produced a brilliant caricature of the elegant, sophisticated Frederic Leighton at an evening reception.

In 1870 the Franco-Prussian war broke out. Following the defeat of France, and the occupation of Paris, Tissot originally remained in the capital. In 1871, however, Tissot fled to England where he had a considerable number of contacts. Tissot was initially the guest of the Editor of Vanity Fair, with whom he had become friendly, and who seems to have opened doors for him both socially and professionally. Tissot, hard working and smart, quickly became successful in London, where his oil paintings of social events and his conversation pieces rapidly became popular. These paintings look beautifully painted and an interesting record of social life at the time, but were controversial. This was the time when commercially successful people were overtaking the landed aristocracy in wealth, and, as patrons of the arts. This situation was not to the liking of everybody, and in some quarters Tissot paintings were regarded as depictions of the nouveau-riche. Ruskin was a particularly severe critic, describing the Tissot paintings as "mere painted photographs of vulgar society." In 1873, the painter bought the house in St John's Wood where he was to live for the rest of his time in London, and he himself started to become a significant figure socially. Tissot's success in London was regarded with envy by Degas and other painters of his circle in Paris.

In the mid 1870s Tissot met Kathleen Newton (1854-1882), an Irish divorcee with a distinctly colourful past. She had formed a sexual relationship with a man on a voyage to India to be married, and borne his child. Kathleen became his model, muse, mistress, and the great love of his life. Tissot's paintings of his lady tell any observer of warmth of his love for her. Many other successful men kept mistresses in St John's Wood, but they did not, like Tissot, live openly with them in adulterous relationships. This situation forced the painter to choose between his social life and Kathleen. To his credit he chose his lady. It would be wrong to thInk that Tissot became something of a solitary person, as he and Kathleen Newton entertained their more bohemian artistic friends at home. But Tissot's days as a man-about-town were over, and he and Kathleen seem to have settled into a quiet life of domesticity. Kathleen's two children lived close by with her sister. Kathleen Newton was an extremely attractive young woman, and appeared in many of Tissot paintings at this time. In the late 1870s her health started to decline, with the beginning of that great 19th century killer Tuberculosis. Tissot remained devoted to her. It is likely that the Roman Catholicism of both paintings would not allow them to contemplate marriage. In 1882, the desperately ill Kathleen cheated consumption by committing suicide, and, as a result was not able to be buried in consecrated ground. With one week Tissot left his home at St Johns Wood, and never returned to it. The house was later bought by Alma-Tadema.

Tissot was devastated by his loss, and never really recovered from it. Tissot seemed unable to accept the enormity and permanence of it. It is rumoured that he considered marriage to other women later in life, but these affairs came to nothing. Like many English people at this time Tissot became interested in Spiritualism, and on a number of occasions tried to contact the dead Kathleen. The exotic French artist and his fallen women-one of the great 19th century English love stories. Initially Tissot carried on working back in Paris, in much the same manner as in London. Tissot produced a series of paintings of attractive, beautifully dressed women in sumptuous surroundings. These paintings were, for a time, extremely fashionable. Following this Tissot experienced a profound religious experience, and became increasingly devout. Tissot embarked on a series of religious paintings, visiting the Middle East on a number of occasions, to observe and paint backgrounds for his oil paintings. These paintings were well-received at the time, but in our more secular age have little appeal.

James Tissot at Buillon died on Friday 8th August 1902.

Paintings, Watercolors and Drawings

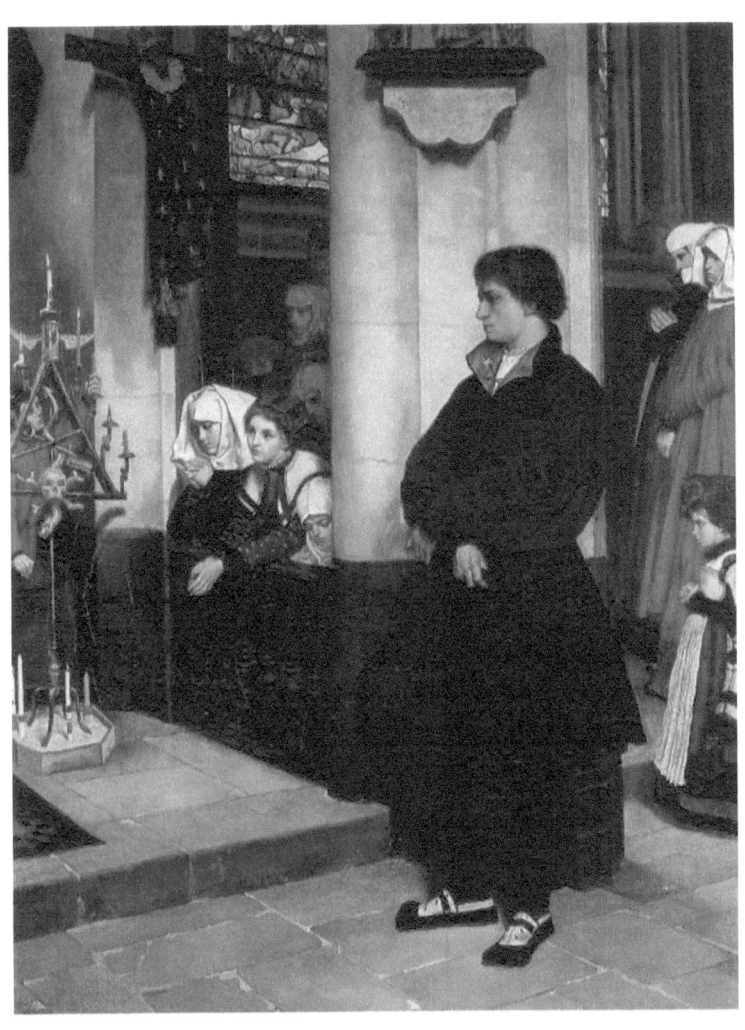

During the Service
1860, oil on canvas

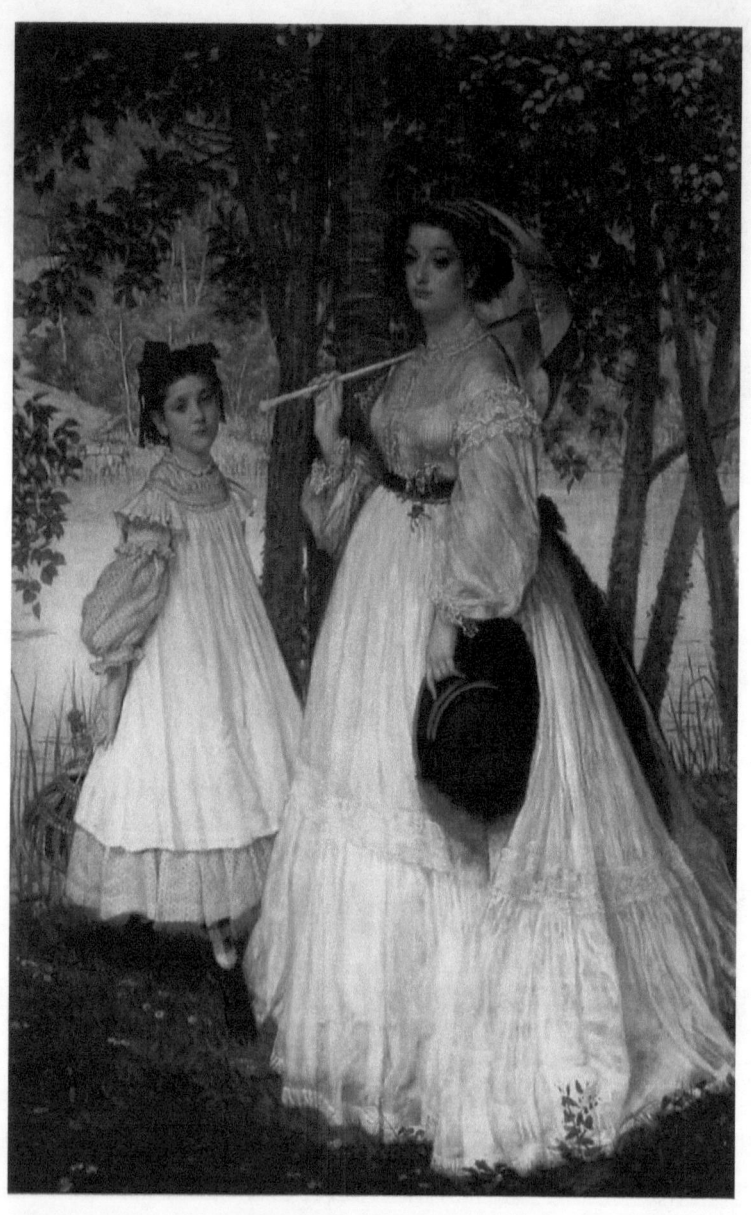

The Two Sisters Portrait
1863, oil on canvas

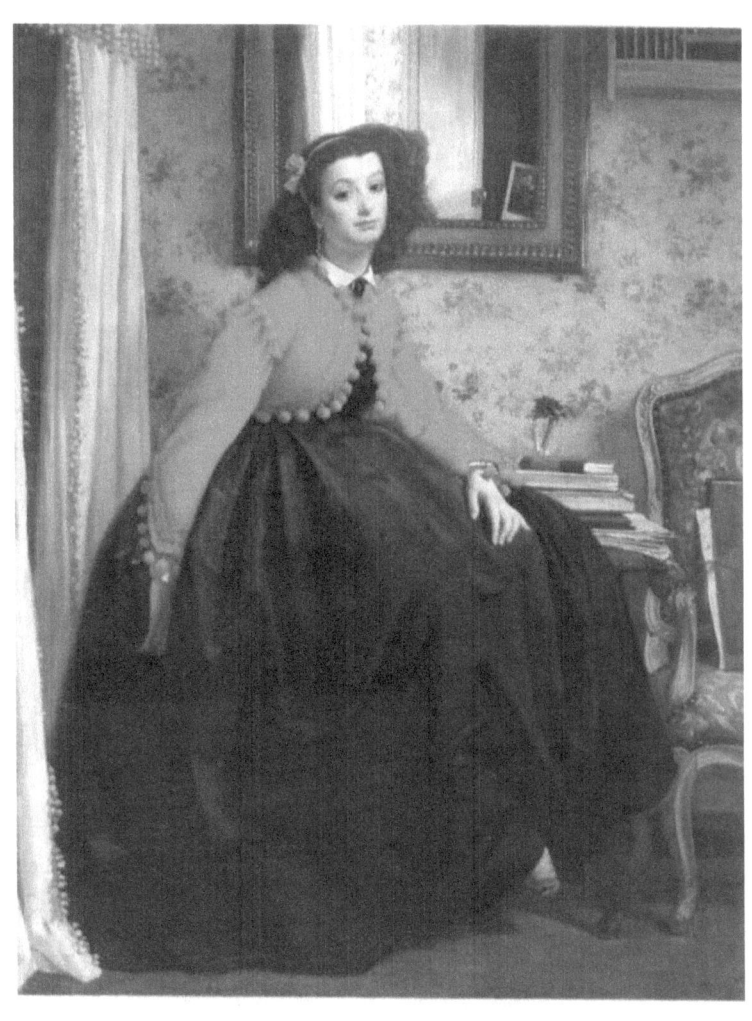

Portrait of Mlle. L.L. (Young Lady in a Red Jacket)
1864, oil on canvas

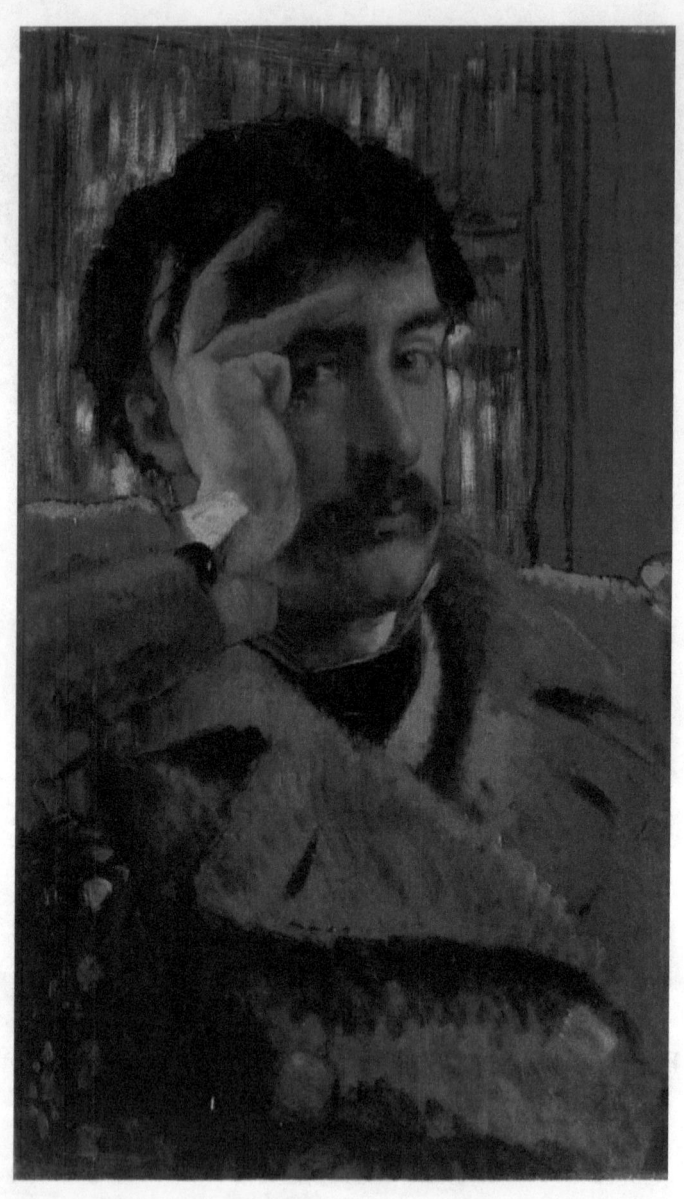

Self Portrait
1865, oil on canvas

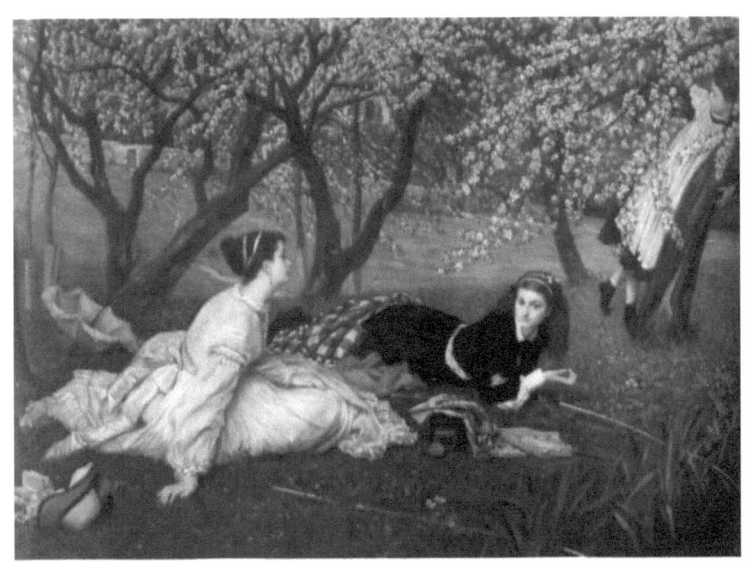

Spring
1865, oil on canvas

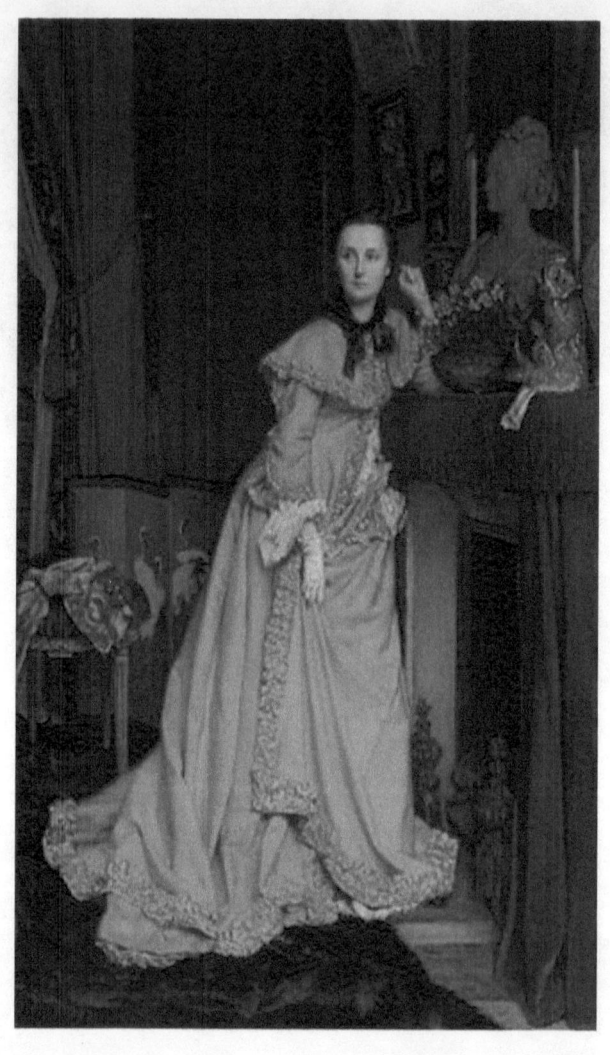

Portrait of the Marquise de Miramon, née, Thérèse
Feuillant
1866, oil on canvas

Costumed in the latest style and surrounded by fashionable decorative objects, the Marquise de Miramon wears a rose colored, ruffled peignoir, or dressing gown. Around her neck are a black lace scarf and a silver cross. Reflecting the new European fascination with Japanese art, behind her is a Japanese screen depicting cranes on a gold ground, and on the mantelpiece are several pieces of Japanese ceramics. The needlework on the Louis XVI stool indicates that the subject is a noble woman of leisure, and the eighteenth-century terracotta bust suggests her husband's aristocratic heritage.

Thérèse -Stephanie-Sophie Feuillant (1836-1912) was from a wealthy bourgeois family. She inherited a fortune from her father and in 1860 she married Réne de Cassagnes de Beaufort, Marquis de Miramon. She stands in the Château de Paulhac, Auvergne, her husband's family seat.

Tissot painted many fashionable women during his career, but he held this work in particularly high regard. In 1866, he wrote to request, and received, permission to borrow the painting and submit it to the Paris World Fair, where it was seen in public for the first time. The family kept this letter from Tissot along with a swatch of the Marquise's pInk velvet gown.

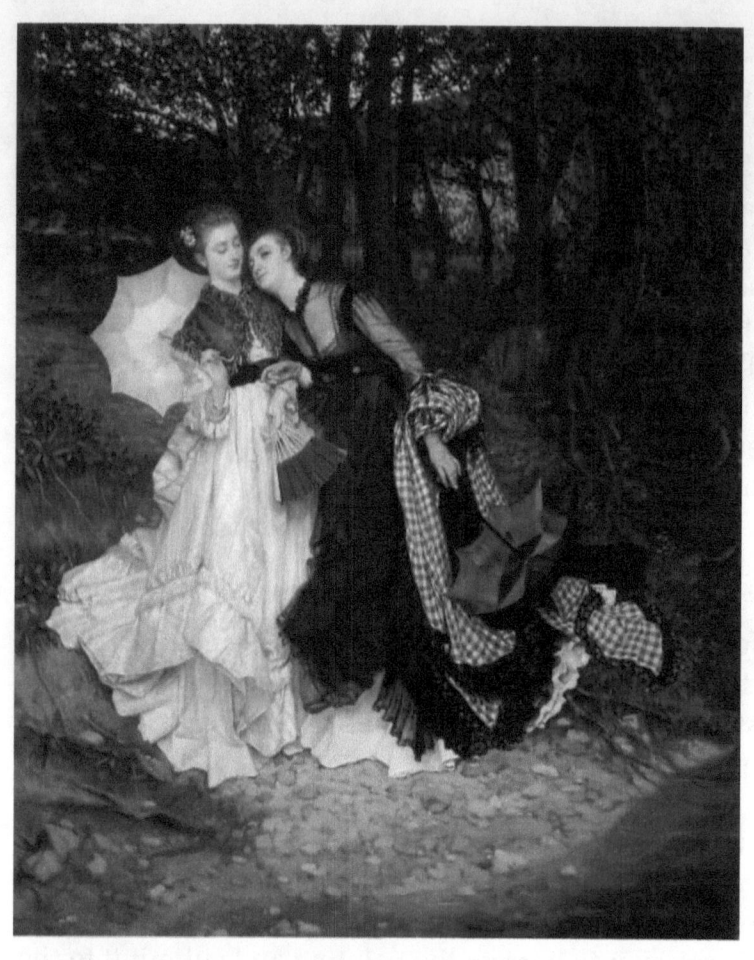

The Confidence
1867, oil on canvas

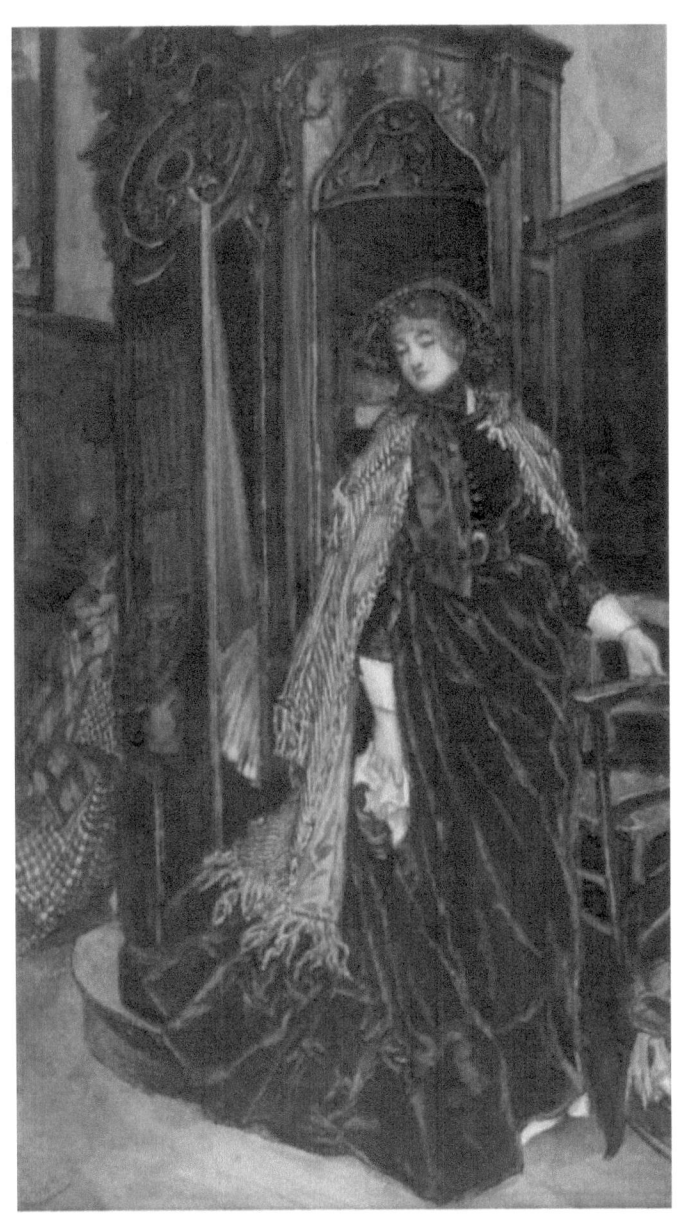

The Confessional
1867, oil on canvas

Tissot painted "The Confessional" during the first stage of his career, before he left Paris and took up residence in London after the Commune in 1871. Although he was a friend of Courbet, Manet, and Degas, his style shows very little of their influence. His work is more descriptive than theirs, and he focused exclusively on the upper echelons of society. Tissot's women were the paradigm of contemporary feminine beauty and grace, against which Degas later rebelled with his piercing analysis of dancers, prostitutes, and bathers. Ostensibly a devotional image, "The Confessional" reads more like a fashion plate. The rich velvet of the woman's dress, satin bow on her hat, stiff lace cuffs, and fine striped shawl with long fringe thrown over her shoulders show her to be a woman of class and refinement. Only the linen handkerchief she holds in her right hand signals any remorse for the sins just confessed.

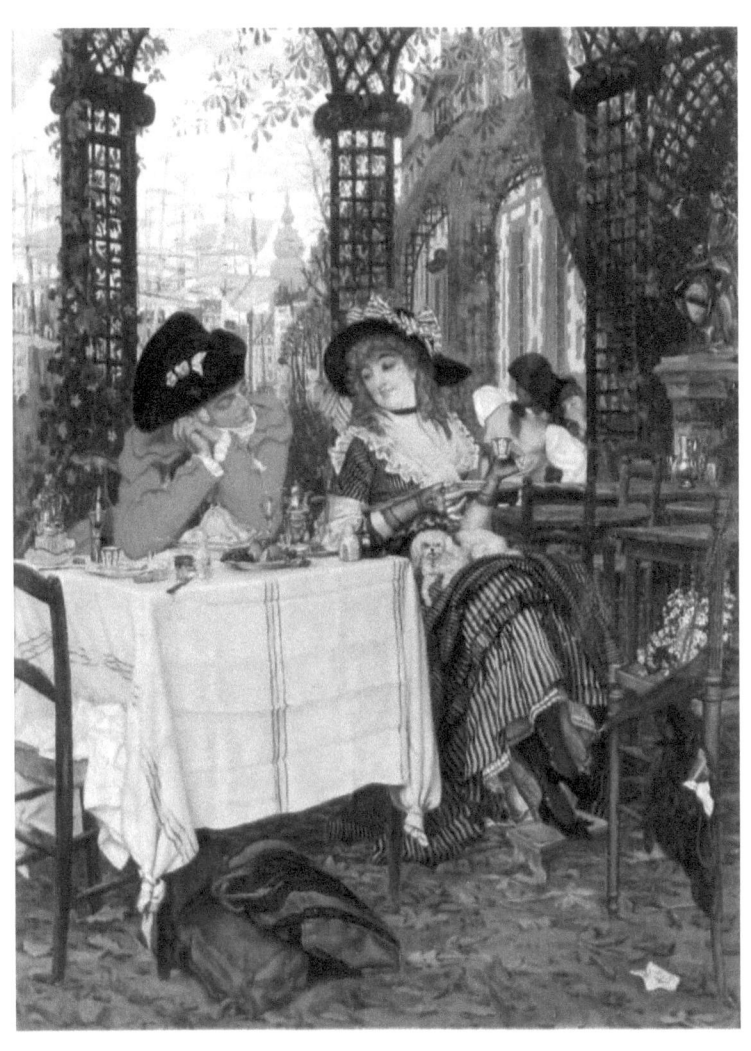

A Luncheon
1868, oil on canvas

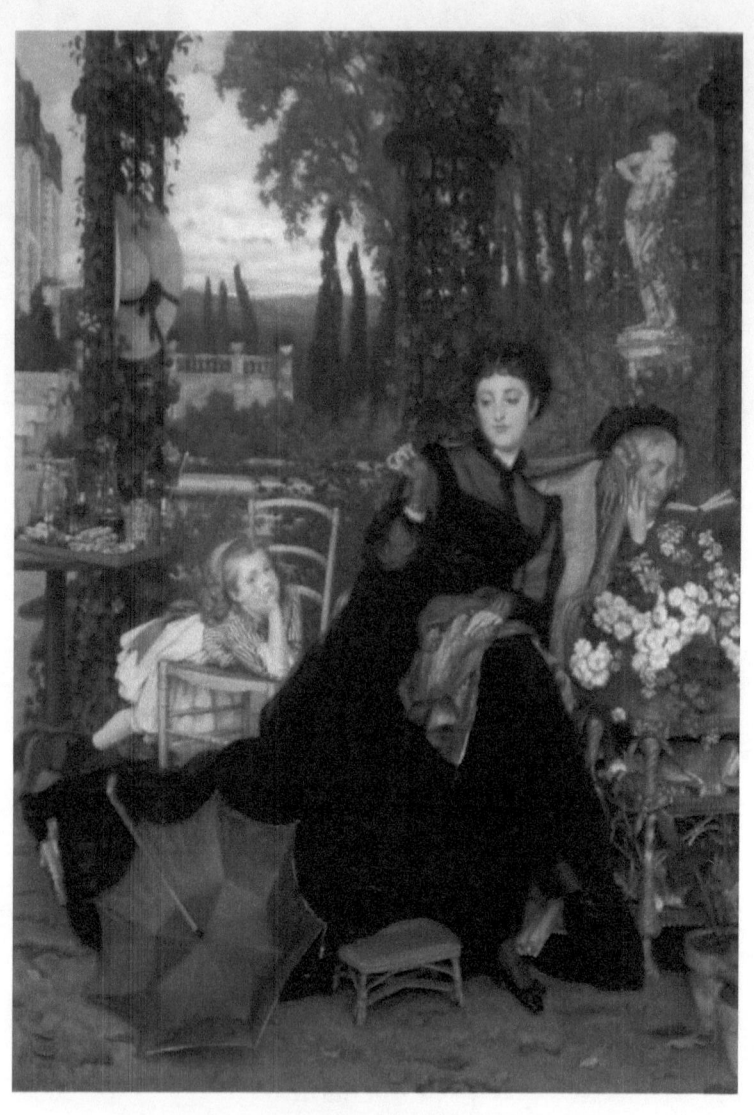

A Widow
1868, oil on canvas

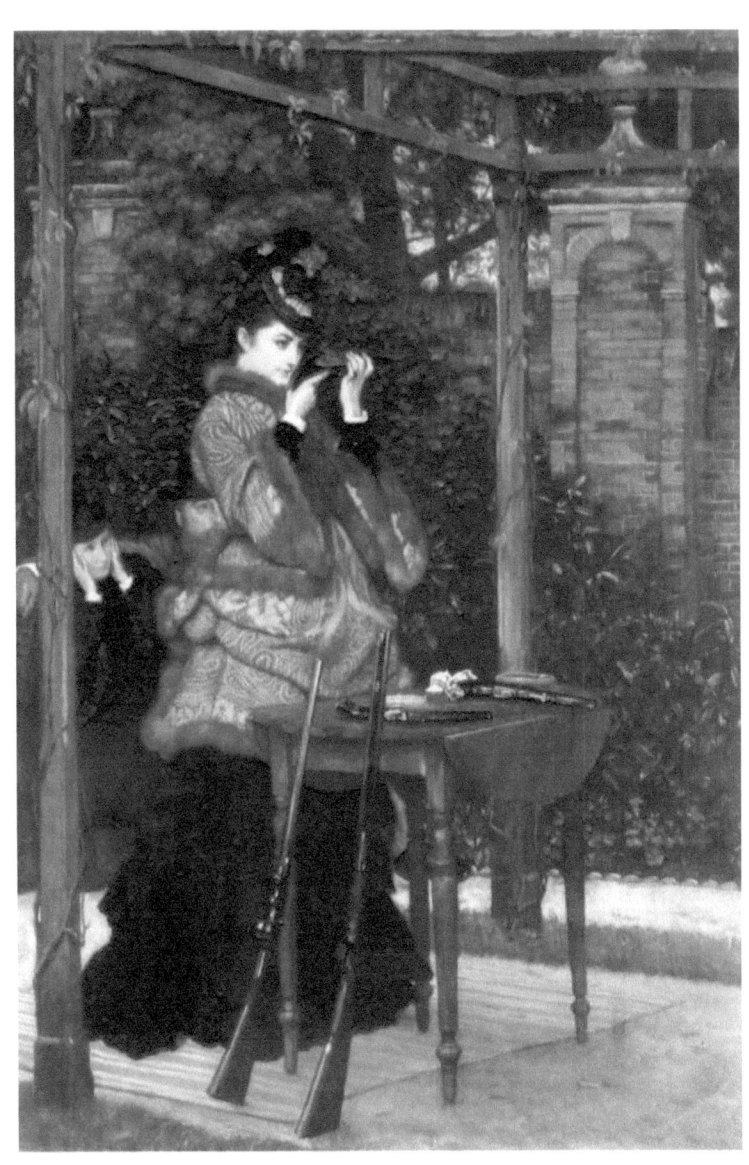

At the Rifle Range
1869, oil on canvas

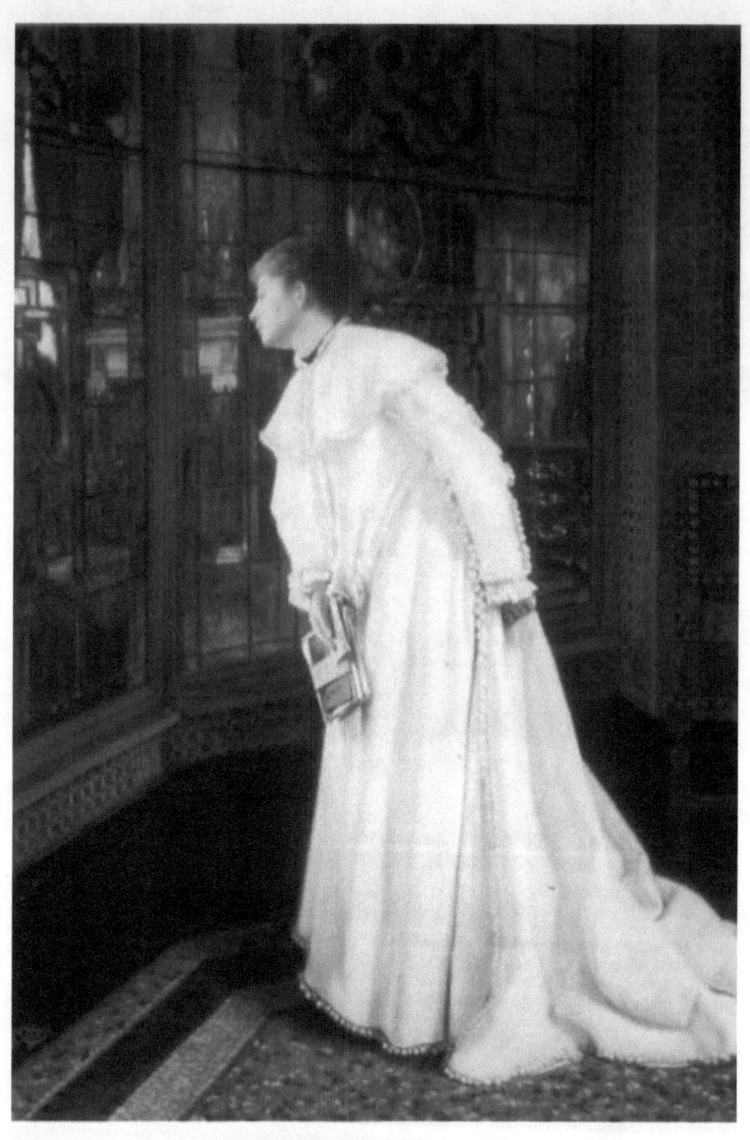

The Stairs
1869, oil on canvas

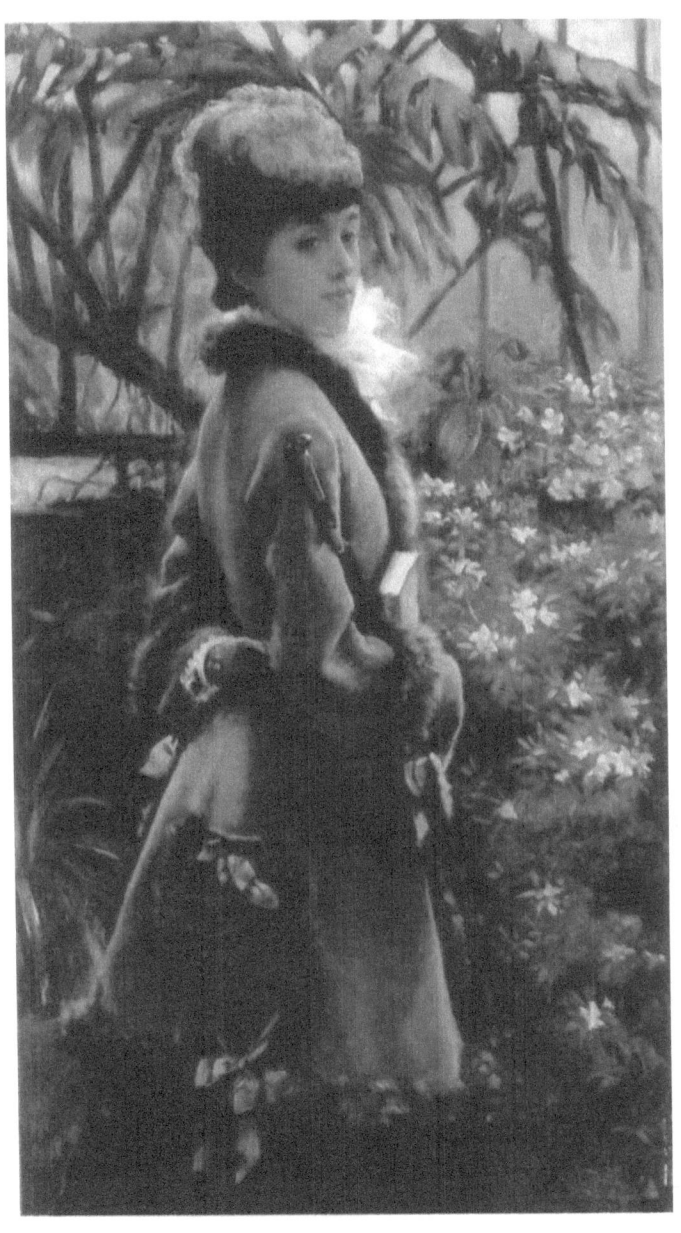

In the greenhouse
1869, oil on canvas

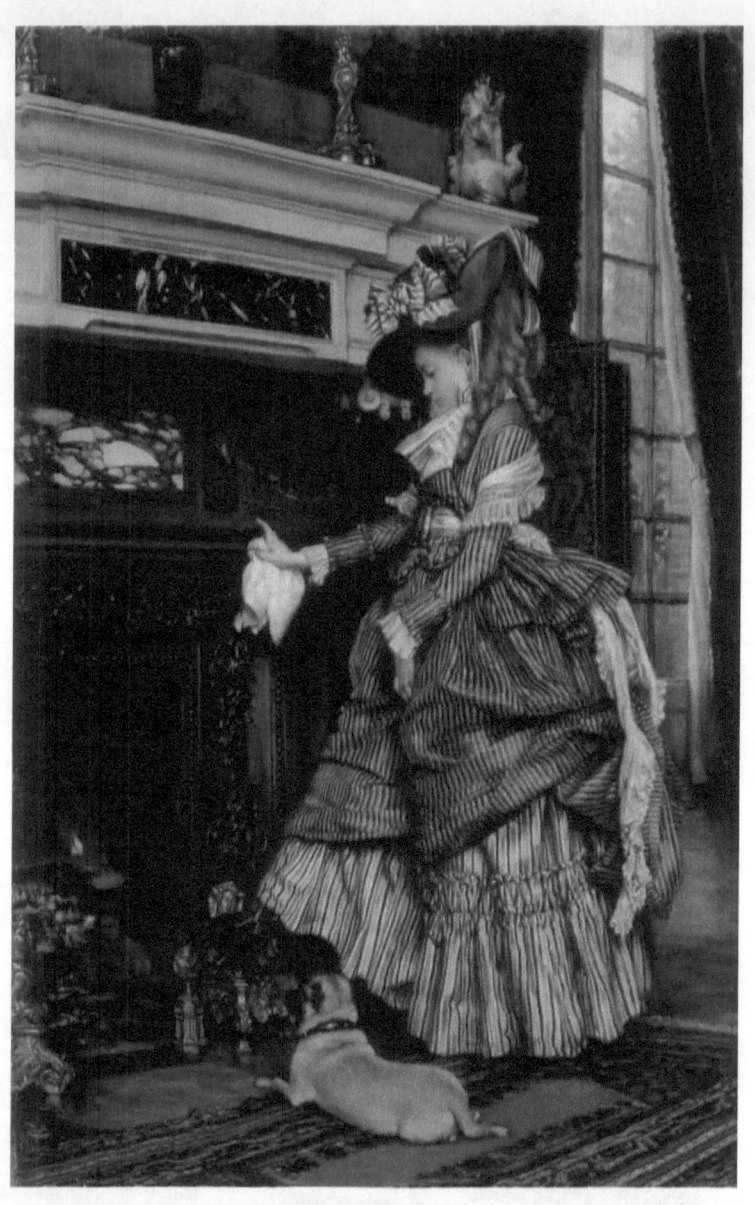

The way
1869, oil on canvas

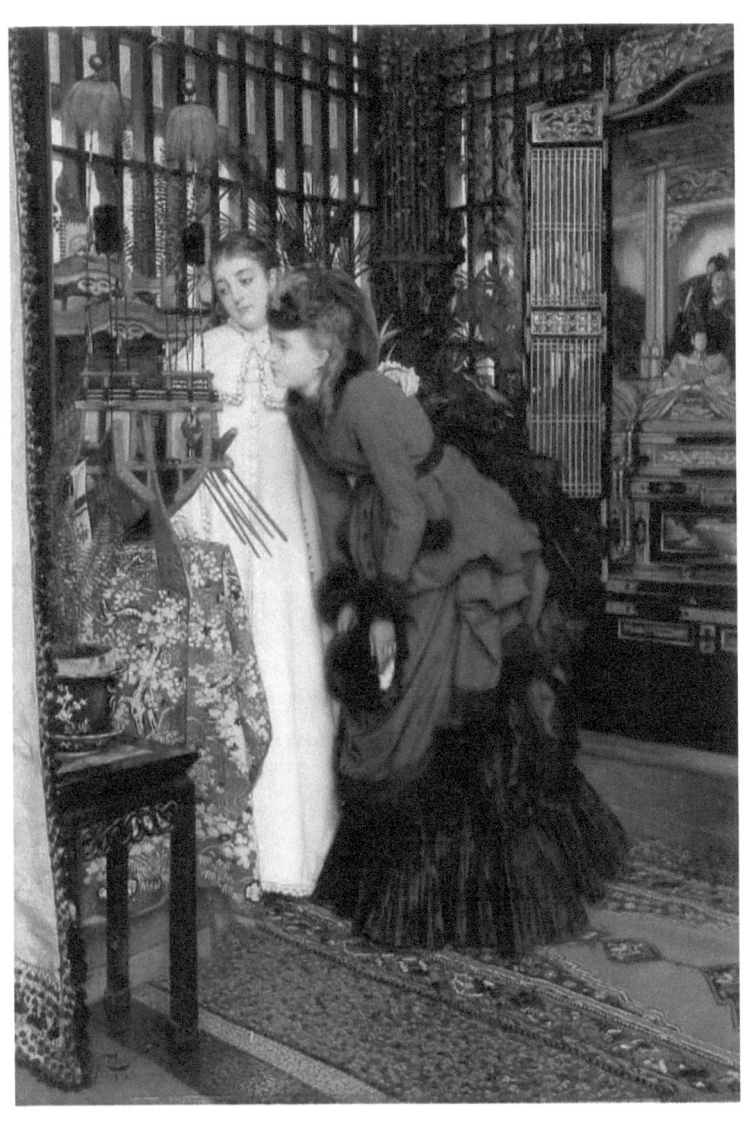

Young Ladies Looking at Japanese Objects
1869, oil on canvas

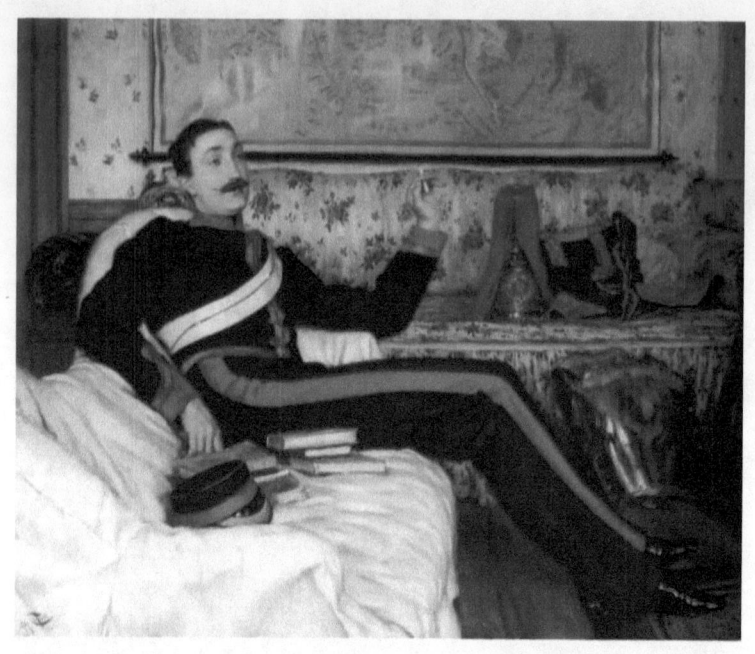

Colonel Frederick Gustavus Barnaby
1870, oil on canvas

An officer of the Royal Horse Guards with a gift for languages and a penchant for travel and exploration, Burnaby became renowned both for his exploits and his writings about them. A Ride to Khiva (1876), the narrative of a journey on horseback across three thousand miles of the Russian steppes in winter, and On Horseback through Asia Minor (1877), which described a tour of Asia Minor during which he fought on behalf of the Turks against the Russians, were both best-sellers. A huge man, nearly two metres (six feet four inches) tall, he was reputed to be the strongest man in the British army and was said to have once carried a pony under one arm. He was painted by Tissot in his uniform as a captain in the 3rd Household Cavalry.

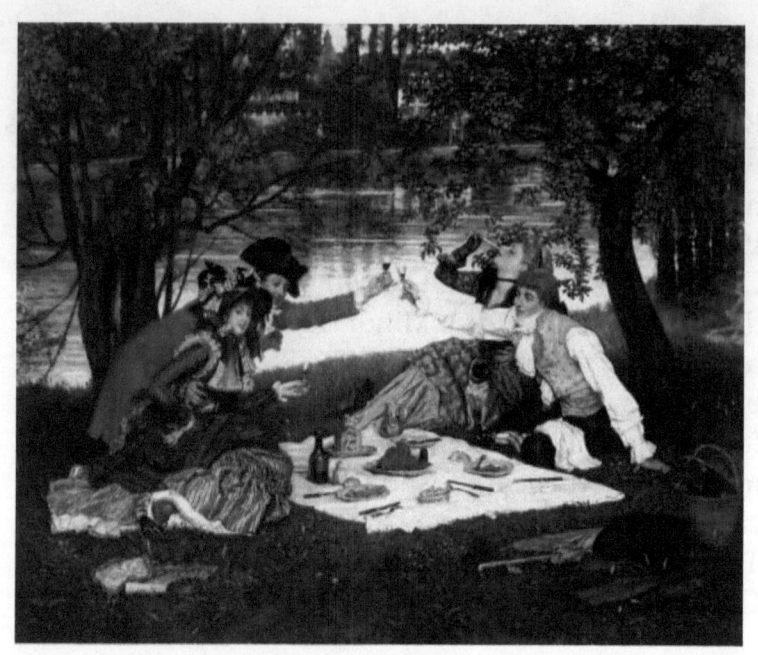

Partie Carree
1870, oil on canvas

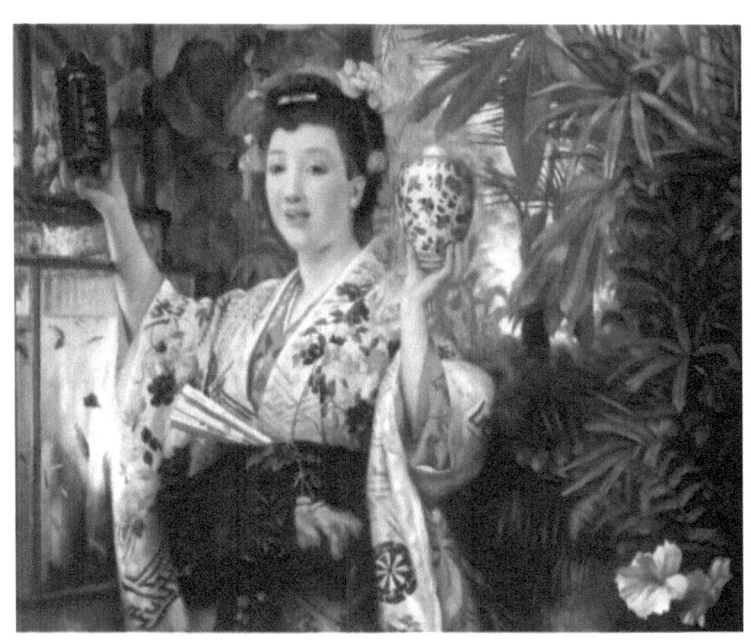

The Japanese Vase
1870, oil on canvas

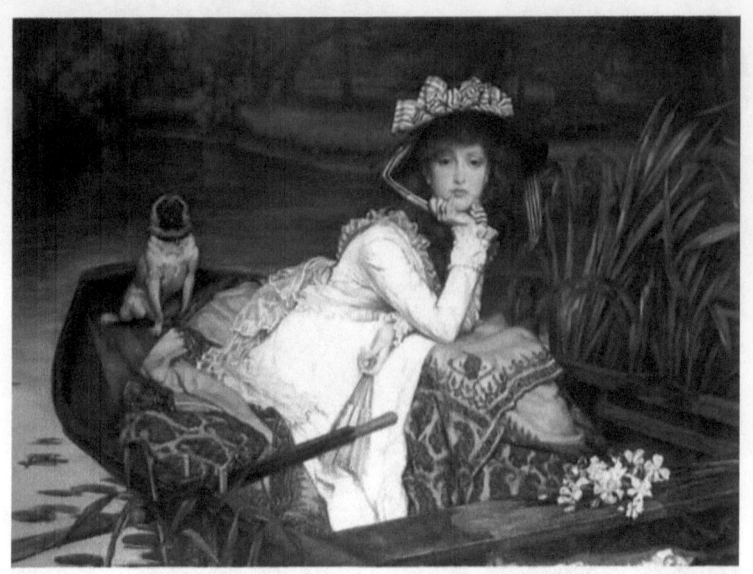

Young Lady In A Boat
1870, oil on canvas

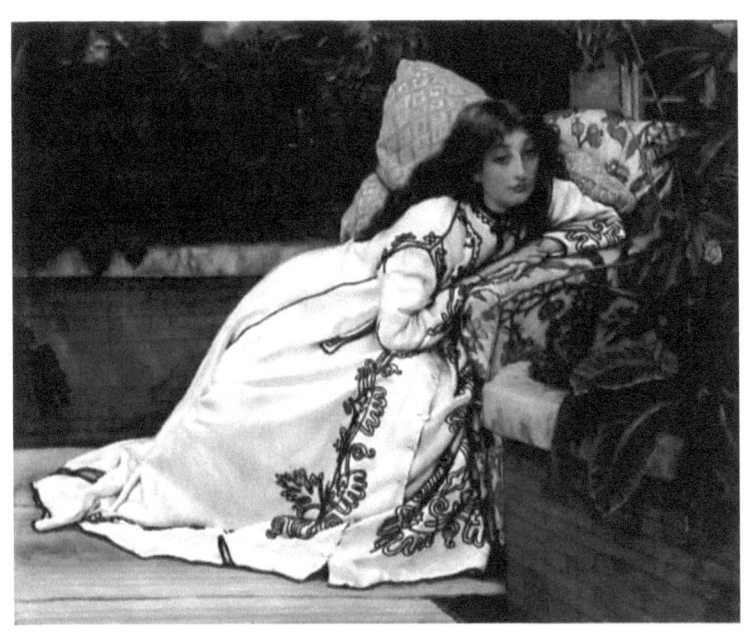

A Girl in an Armchair
1872, oil on canvas

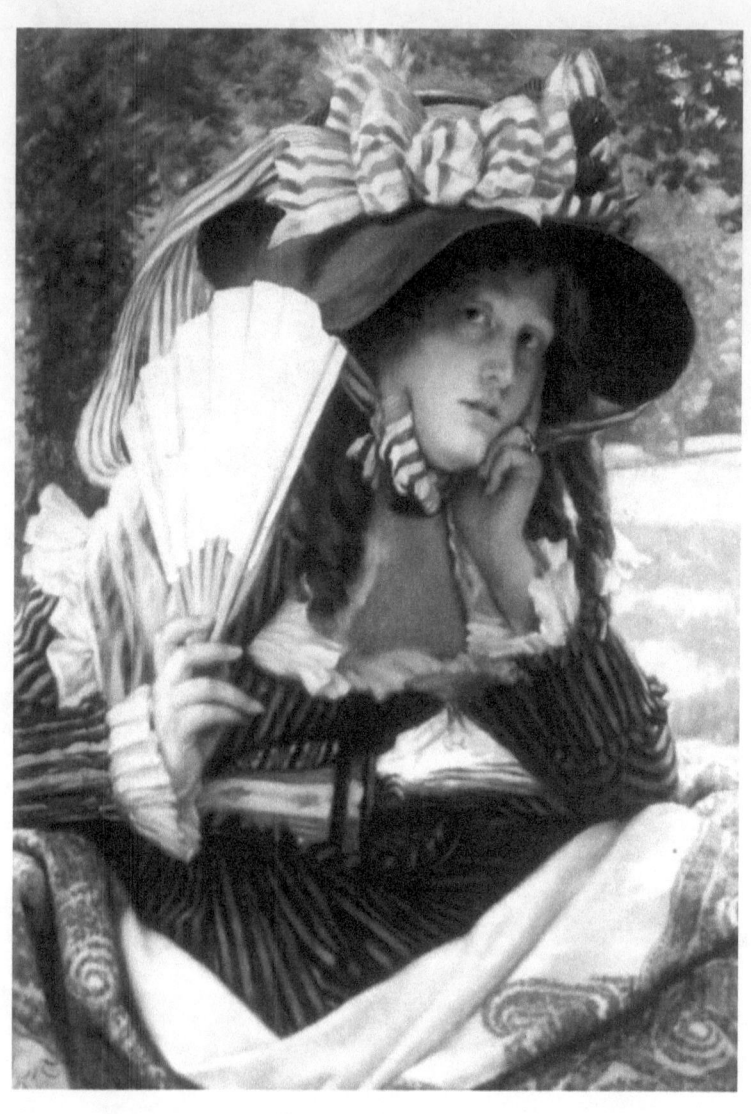

Girl with a fan
1871, oil on canvas

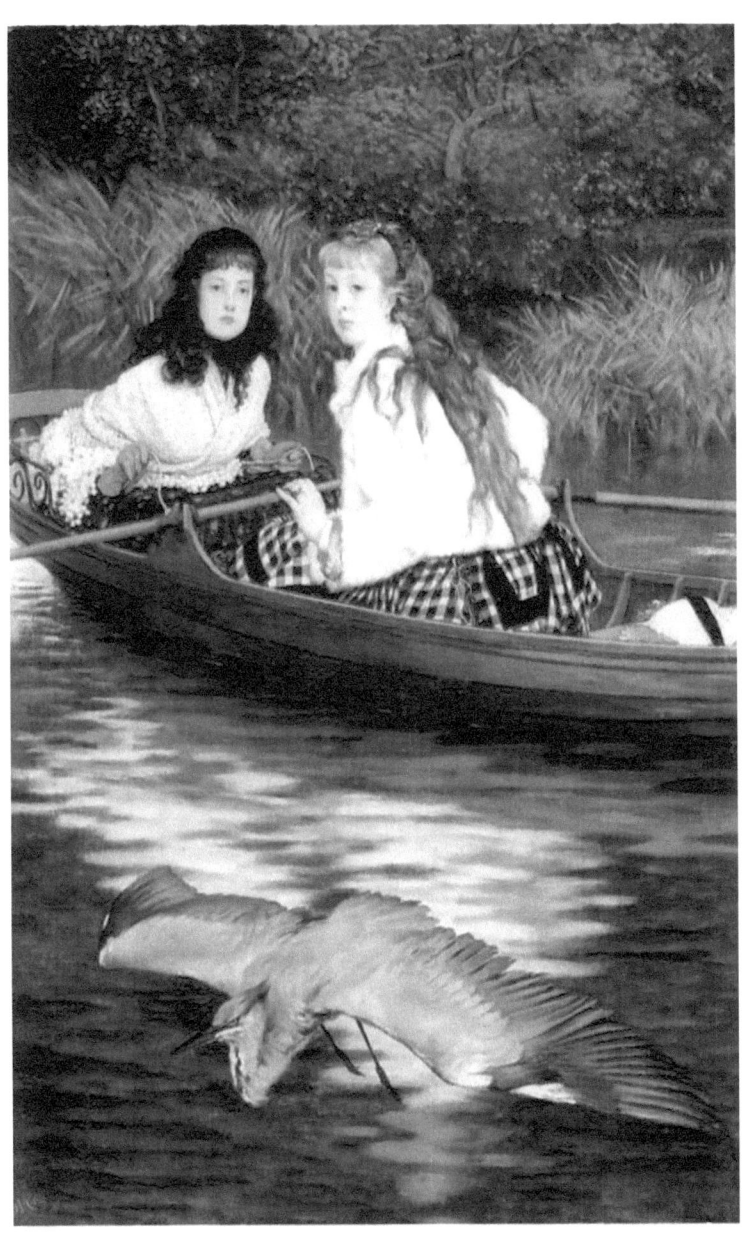

On the Thames, a Heron
1871, oil on canvas

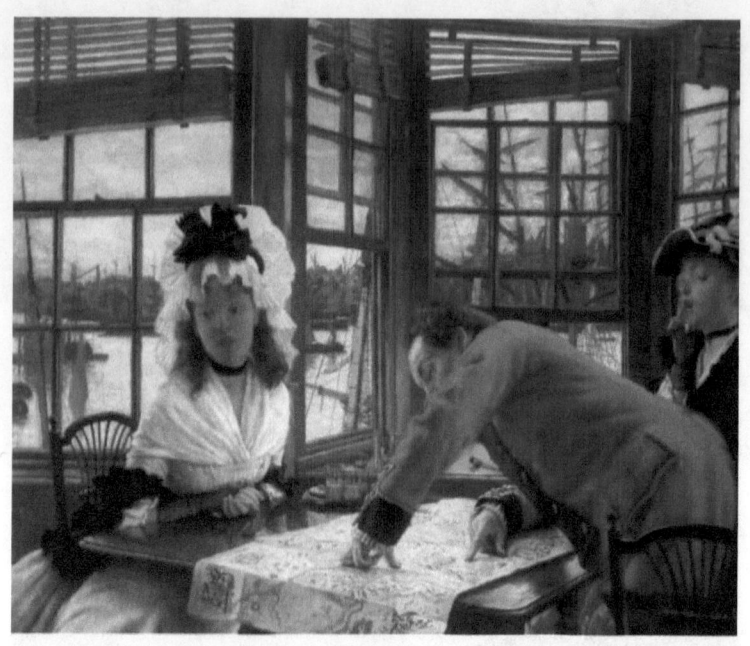

An Interesting Story
1872, oil on canvas

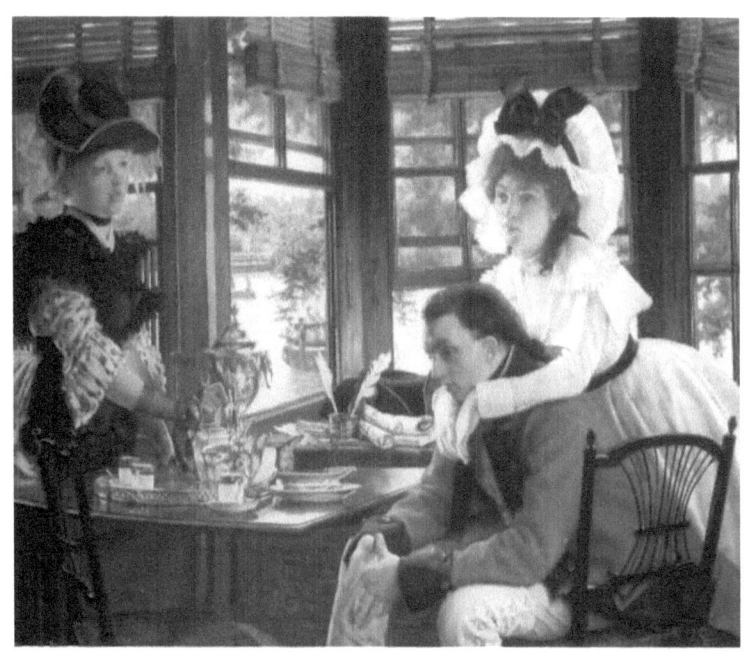

Bad News
1872, oil on canvas

Born in Nantes, Tissot studied in Paris and spent the years 1871-82 in England. He occupies a place in the British 'Modern Life' genre movement, as well as a position on the fringes of French Impressionism. This is one of a series of pictures inspired by eighteenth-century British art, which rearrange costumed models and props before a landscape viewed through a bay window. In 1874 Tissot had such a bay window installed in his London studio.

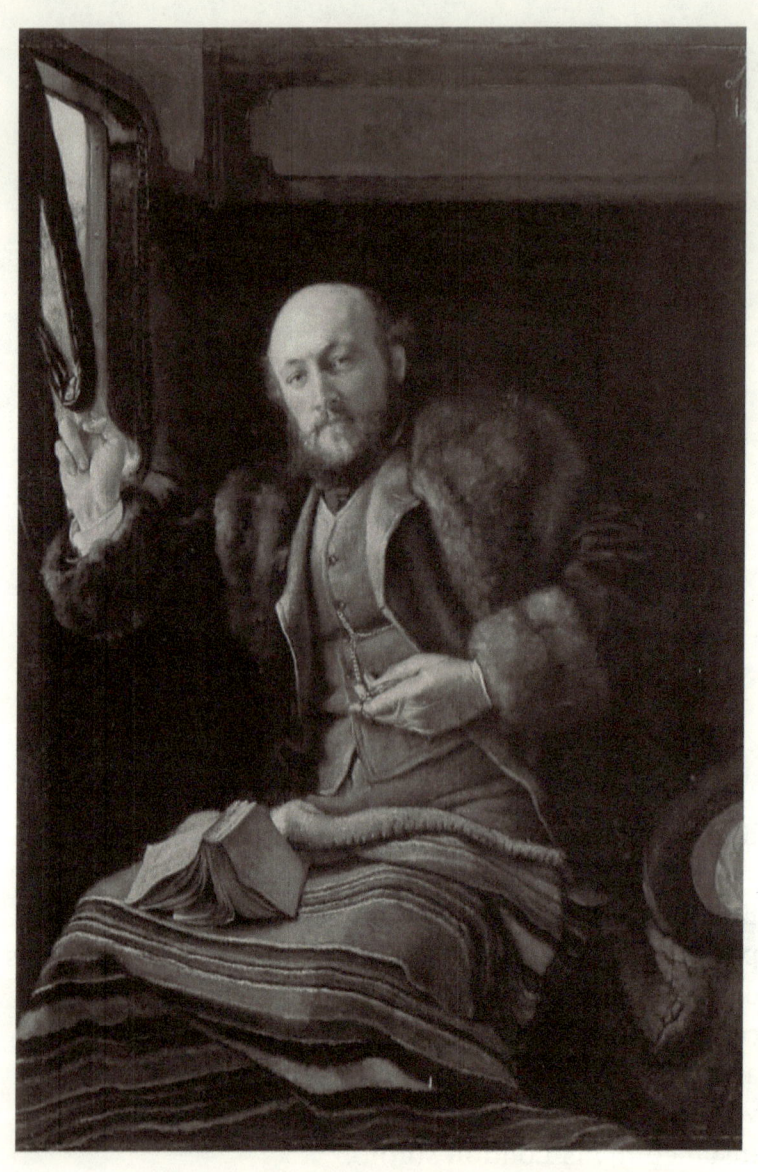

Gentleman in A Railway Carriage
1872, oil on canvas

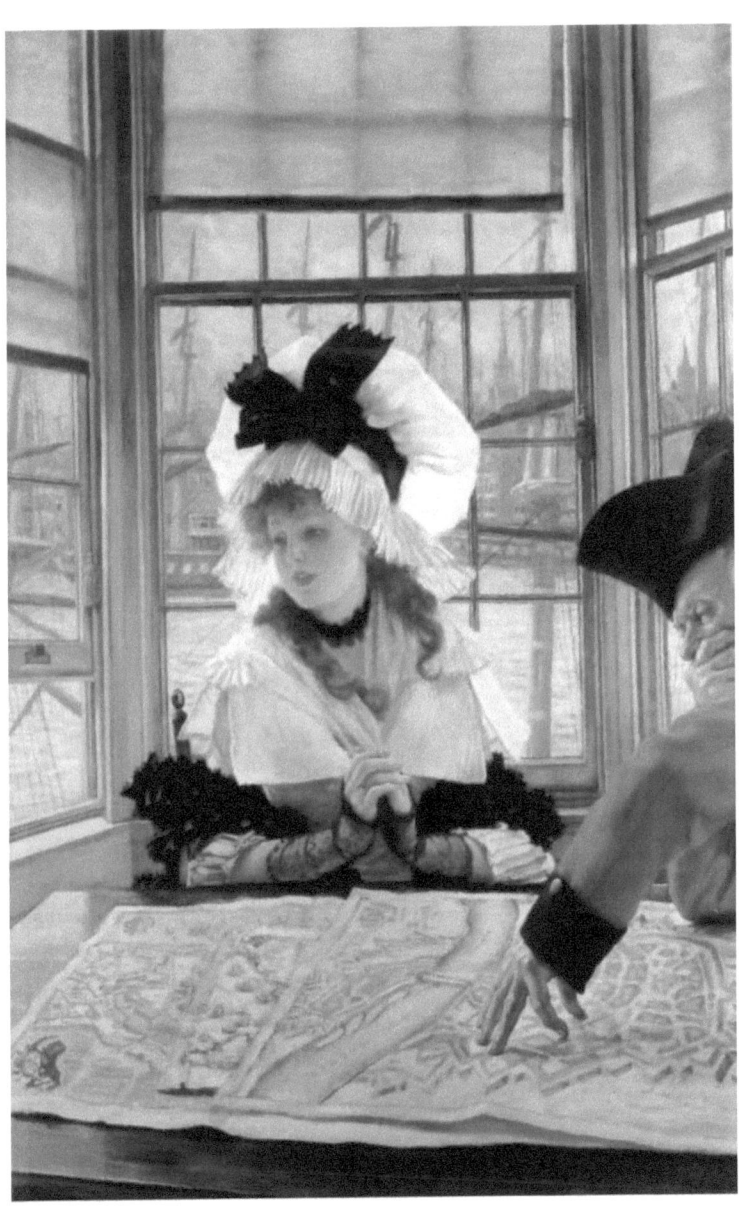

The Tedious Story
1872, oil on canvas

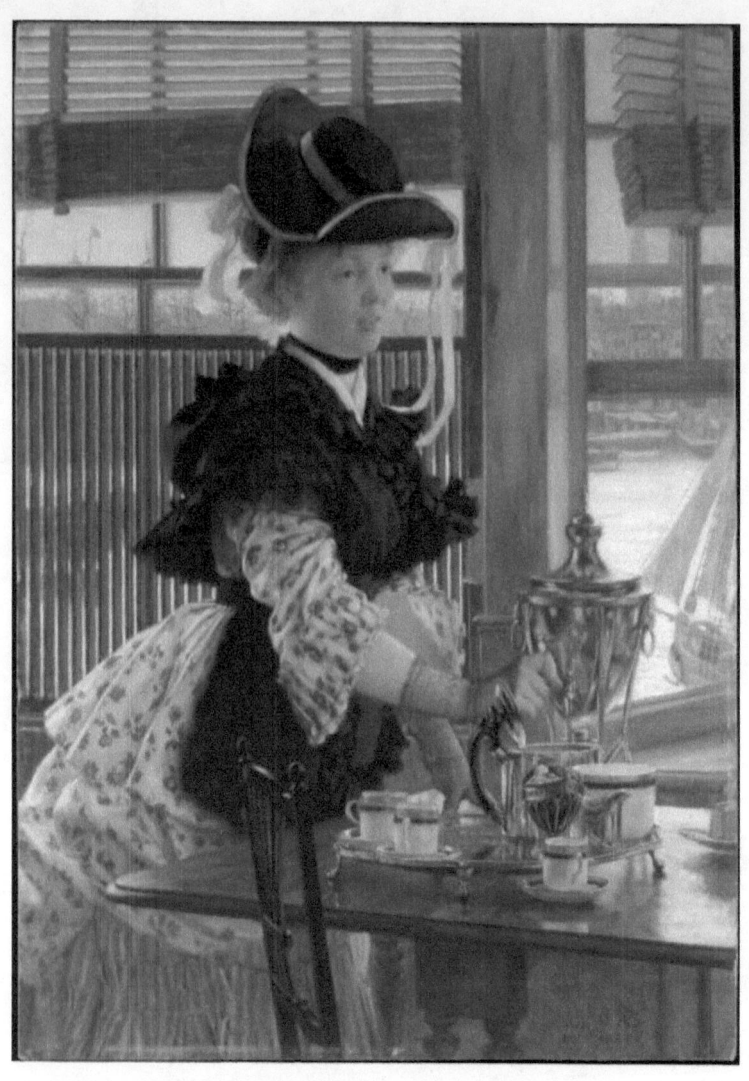

Tea
1872, oil on canvas

When Tissot moved to London in 1871, he immersed himself in the local scene, with work for "Vanity Fair" and genre paintings with the river Thames as backdrop. "Tea" is a repetition of the left-hand portion of one of his most famous London scenes, "Bad News" (National Museum of Wales, Cardiff), which shows a captain and his girlfriend absorbing the news of his imminent departure while a companion prepares tea.

"Bad News" shows the Pool of London through the tavern windows, while "Tea" displays the dense London cityscape beyond that stretch of the river. Tissot's friend Edgar Degas owned a pencil study for this picture.

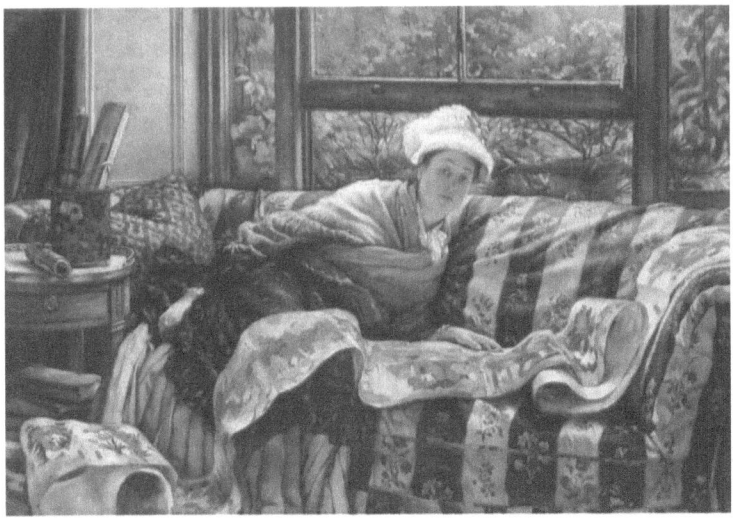

The Japanese Scroll
1872-73, oil on panel

The Japanese Scroll is set in Tissot's London home, Springfield Road (now demolished), where he lived for a year from March 1872 to 1873, or his new Grove End Road house nearby. The forest of greenery in the St John's Wood garden, beyond the sash window, with blossoming flowers including exotic azaleas, casts a cool light into the room. The blue-and-white-striped fabric, with alternating color flower sprigs, is a type inspired by eighteenth-century examples and very fashionable at the time in France. Tissot's passion for eighteenth-century decorative arts and costume matched his interest in oriental objects, and is reflected also in the small oval table by the settee and in the embroidered yellow shawl worn by the young woman. Furniture, ceramics and glassware in Tissot's London pictures of the early 1870s show that he accumulated an array of eighteenth-century items, continuing a collecting interest he had pursued in Paris. The Japanese scrolls in this painting, and the colorful cloisonné enamel pot holding some of them unopened, indicate that Tissot also continued to pursue his love of Japanese art in London. He also had oriental ceramics, furniture, embroidered textiles, screens, masks and parasols, which appear in various paintings and prints created during his London stay. The Japanese Scroll, however, is the only known London painting to focus on a Japanese object.

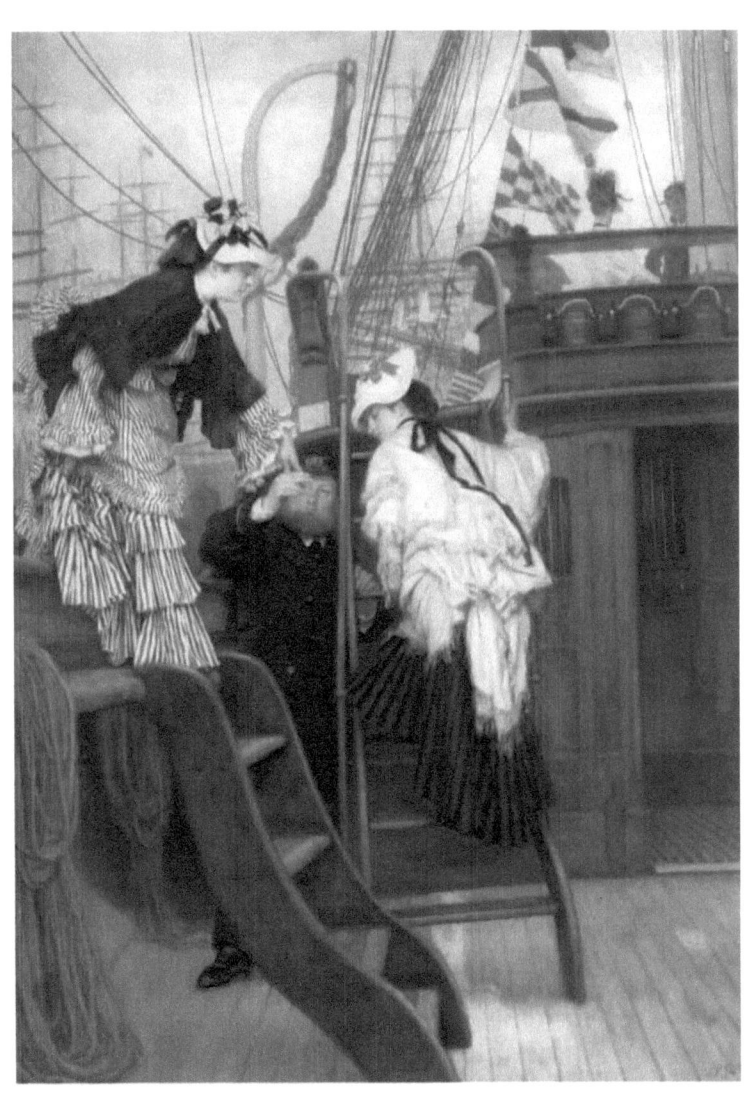

Boarding the Yacht
1873, oil on canvas

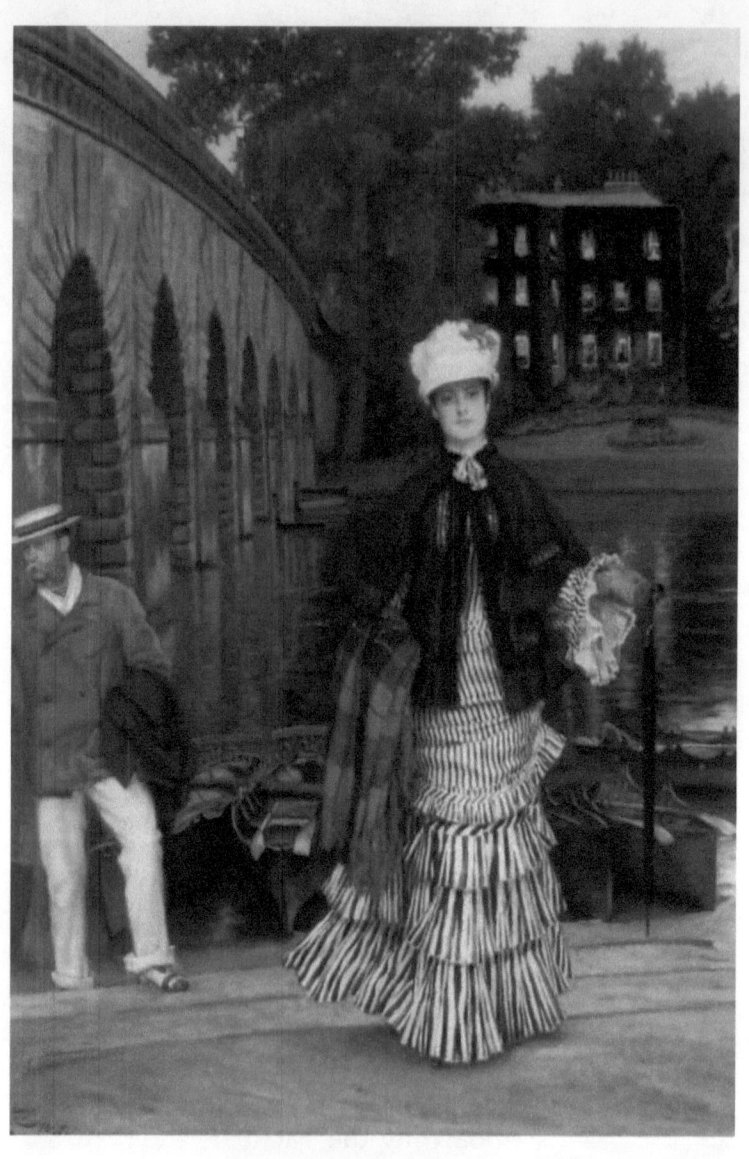

The Return from the Boating Trip
1873, oil on canvas

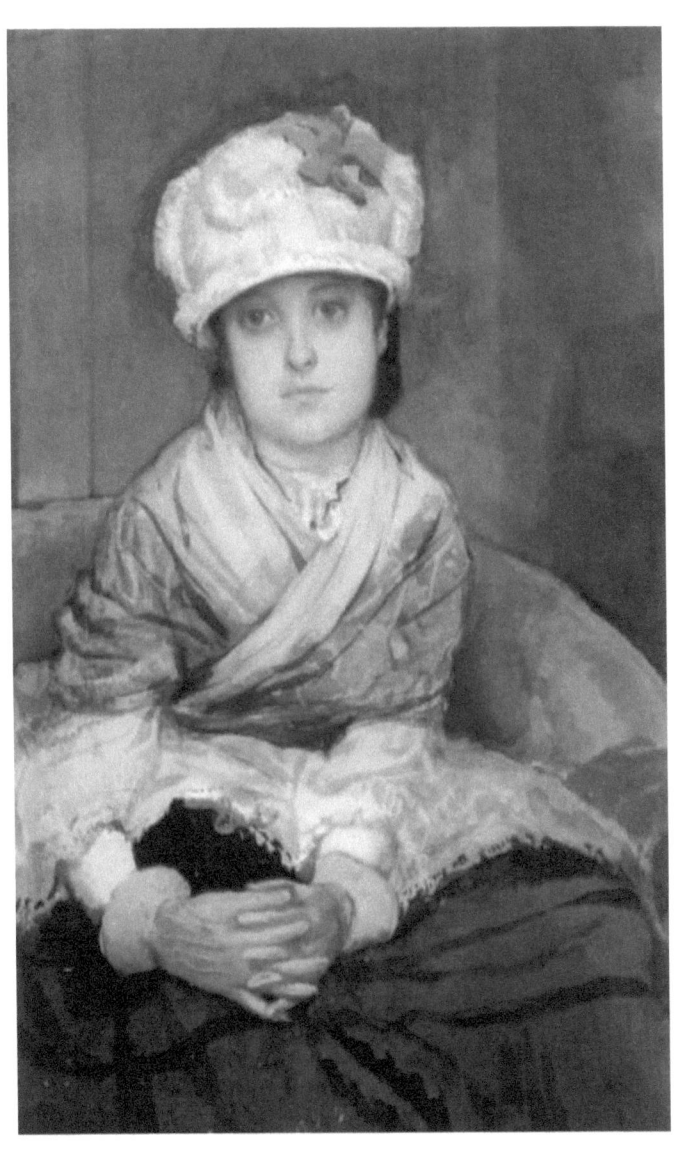

Waiting, 1873
Watercolor

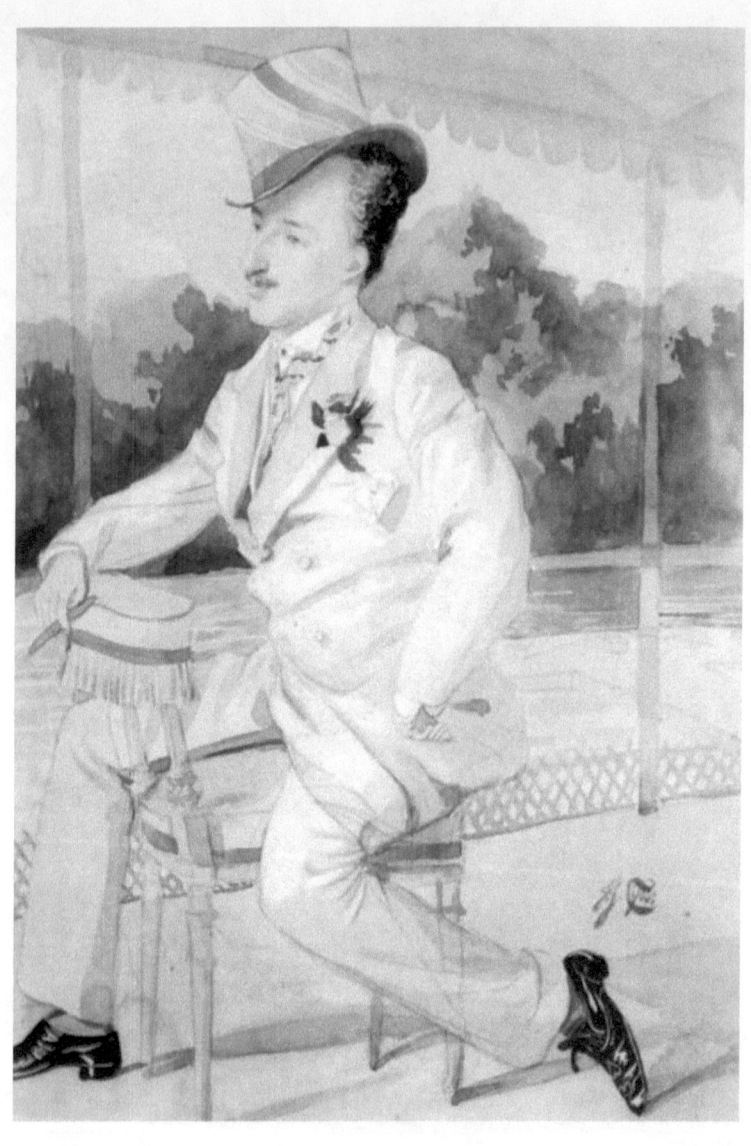

A Dandy, 1871-1873
Watercolor

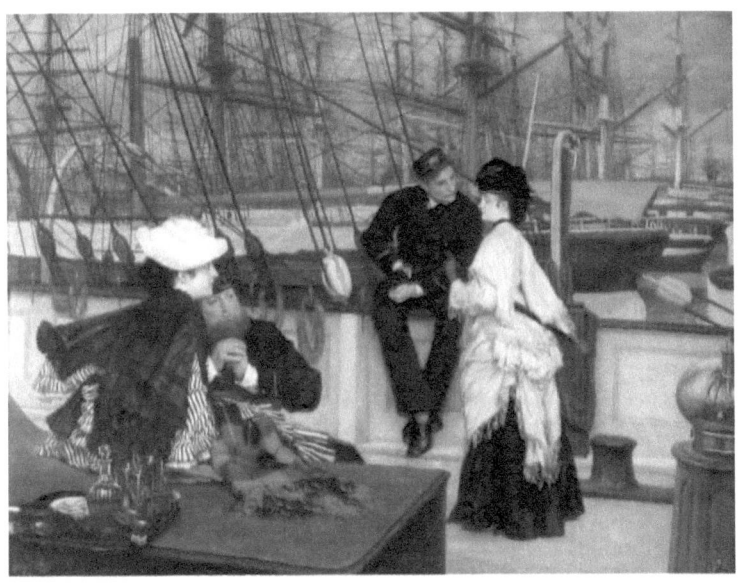

The Captain and the Mate , 1873, oil on canvas

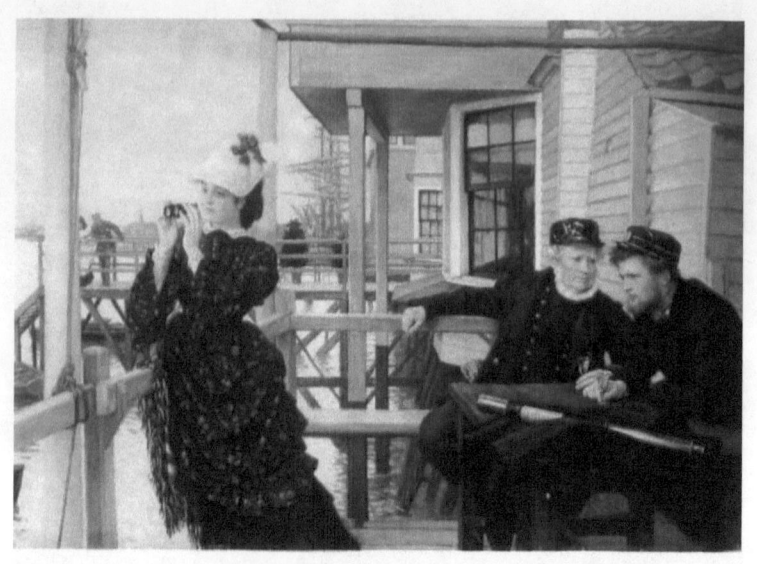

The Captain's Daughter , 1873, oil on canvas

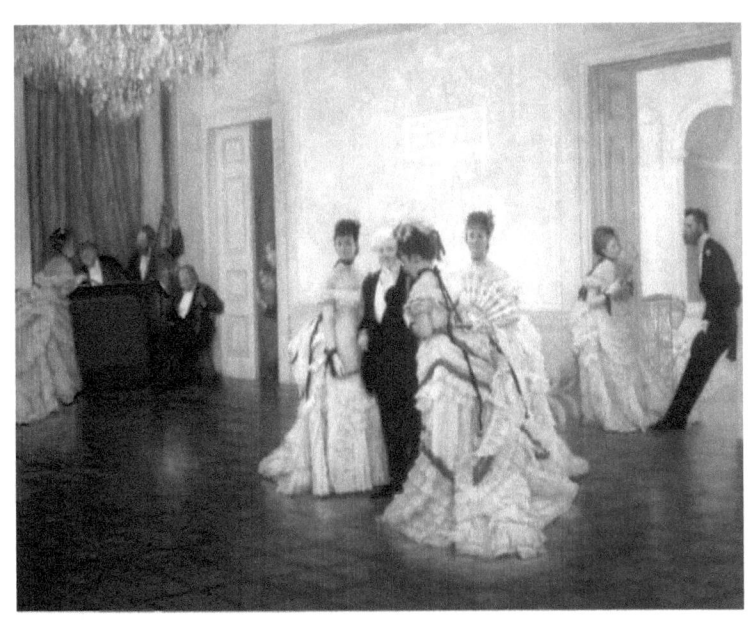

Too Early
1873, oil on canvas

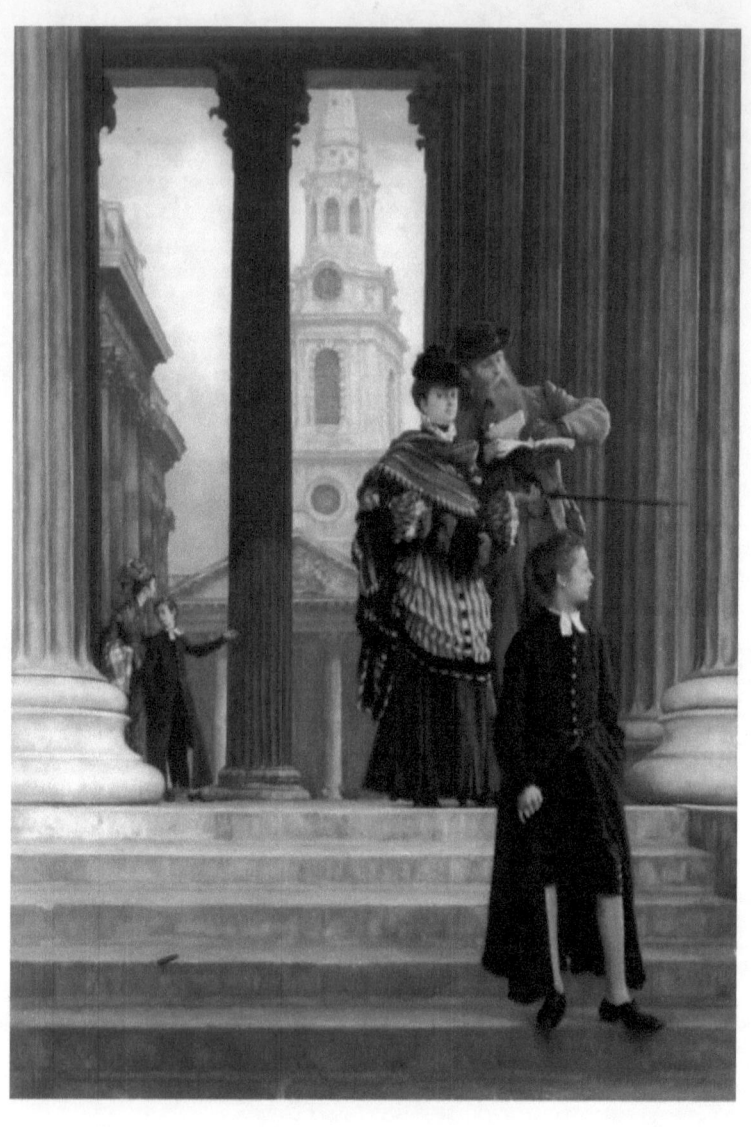

London Visitors
1874, oil on canvas

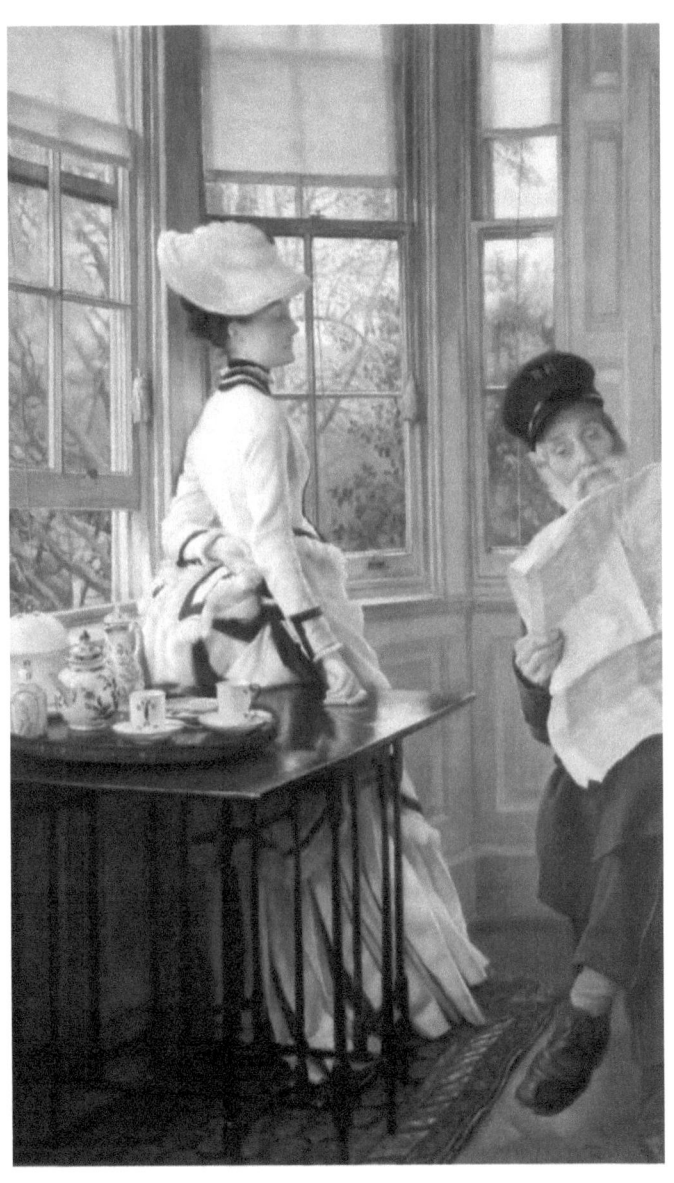

Reading the News
1874, oil on canvas

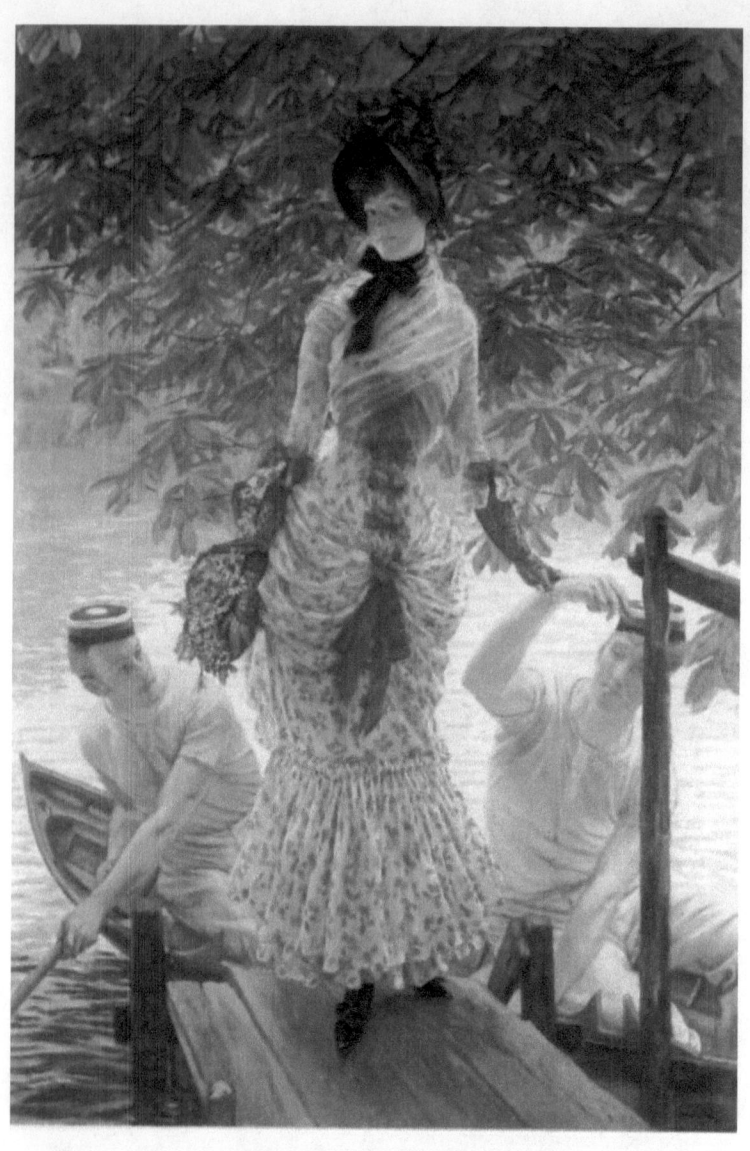

On the Thames
1874, oil on canvas

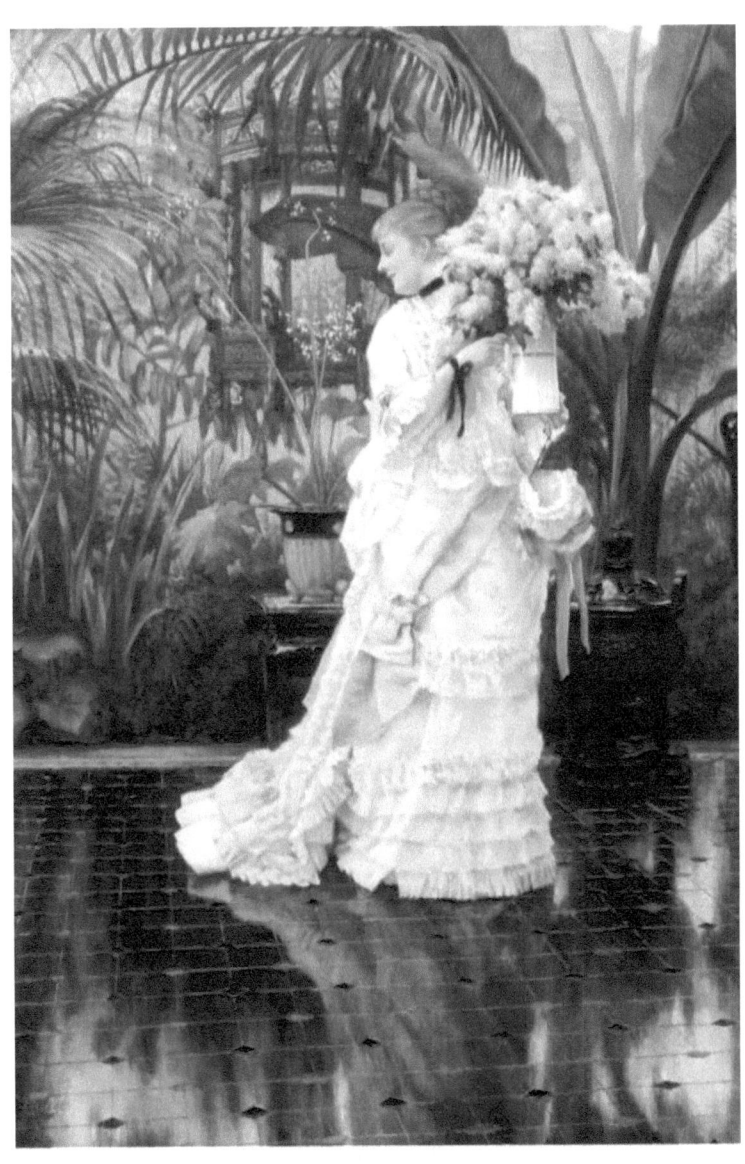

The Bunch of Lilacs
1875, oil on canvas

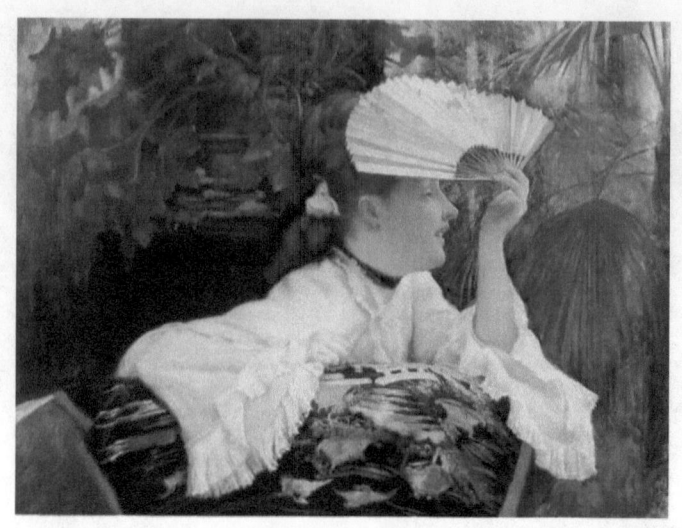

The Fan
1875, oil on canvas

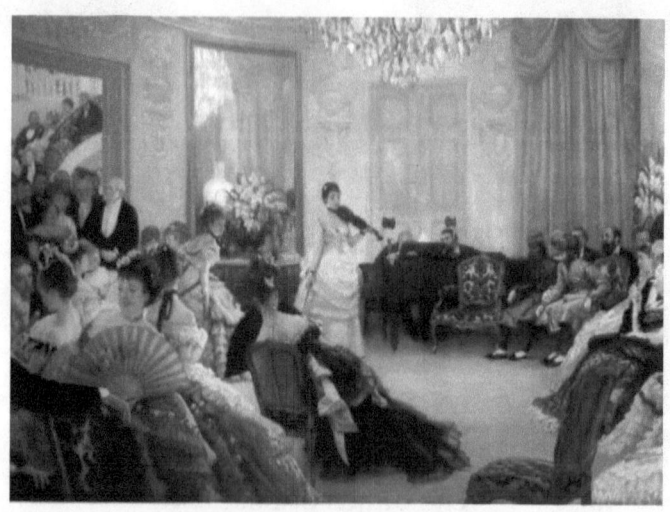

Hush! (The Concert)
1875, oil on canvas

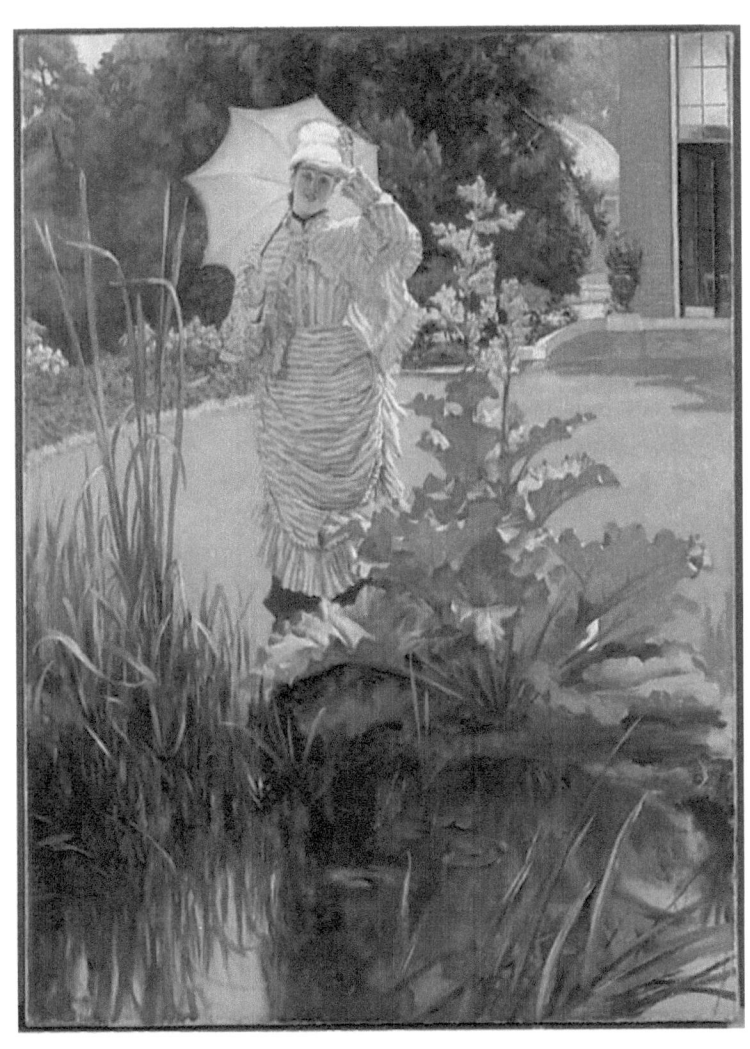

Spring Morning
1875, oil on canvas

Tissot was an early and avid aficionado of Japanese woodblock prints, from which silhouetted figure and the prominent clump of vegetation in this work are thought to derive. Until this painting reappeared at auction in 1981, its composition was known for only by means of a related drypoint. When that print was exhibited in London, in 1876, it was inexplicably singled out by a critic who described it as "intensely vulgar, but clever enough for the public it appeals to."

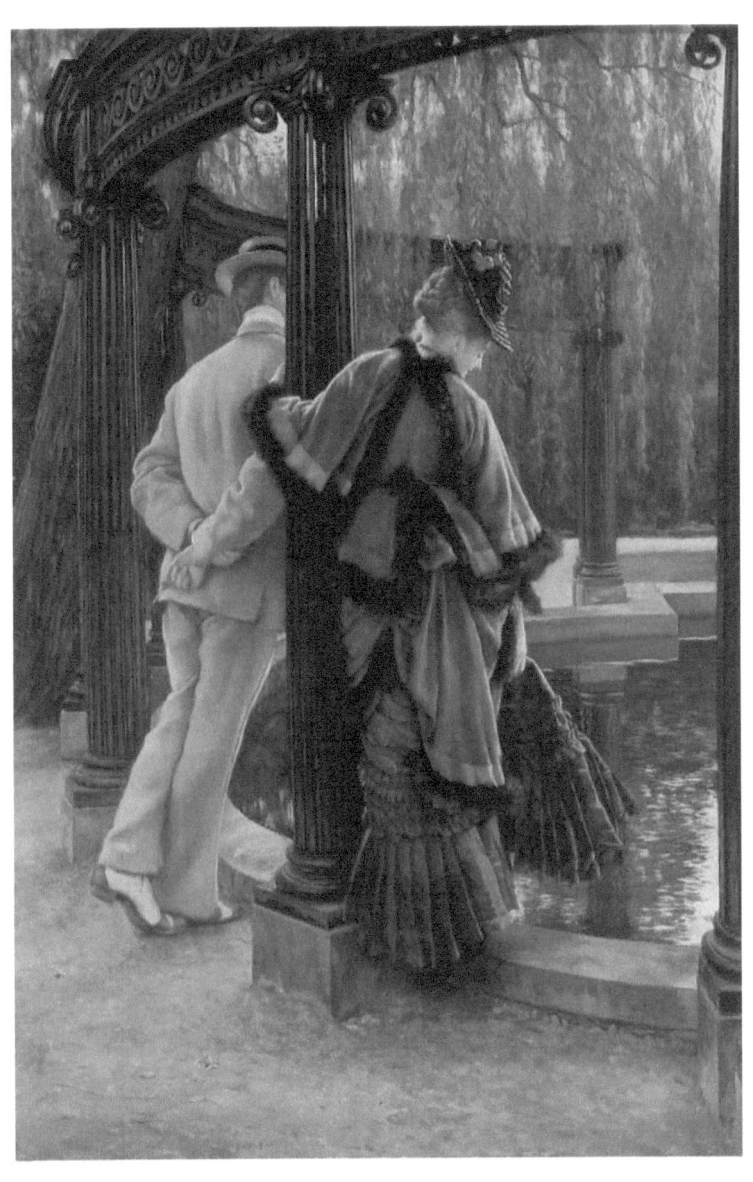

Quarrelling
1876, oil on canvas

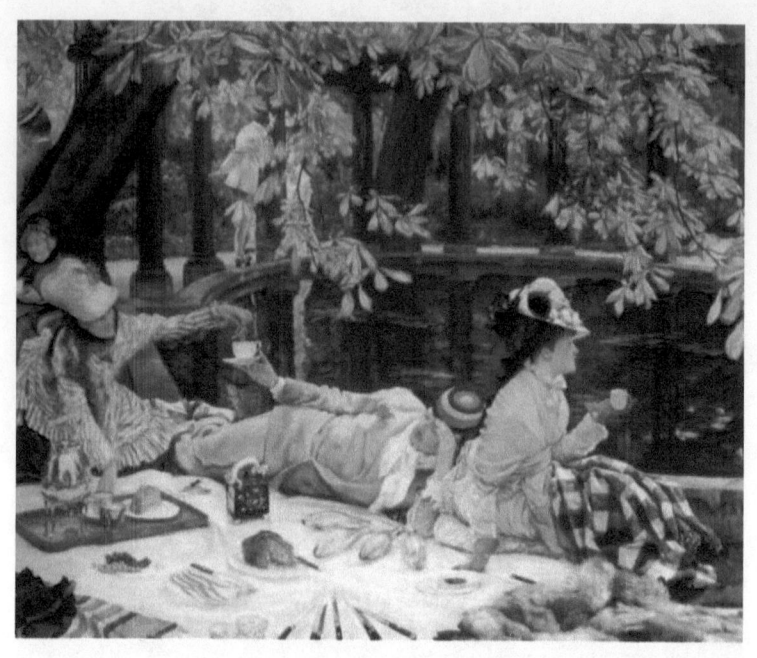

Holyday
1876, oil on canvas

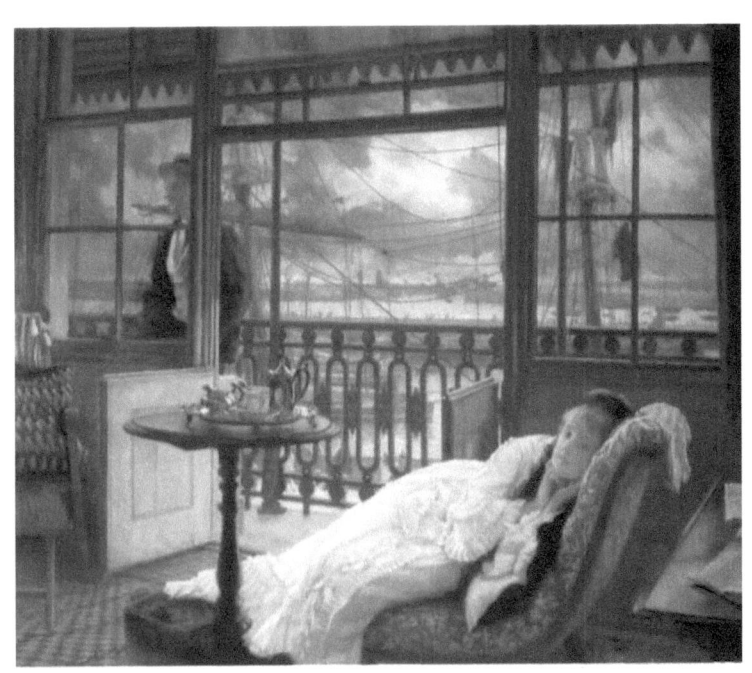

A Passing Storm
1876, oil on canvas

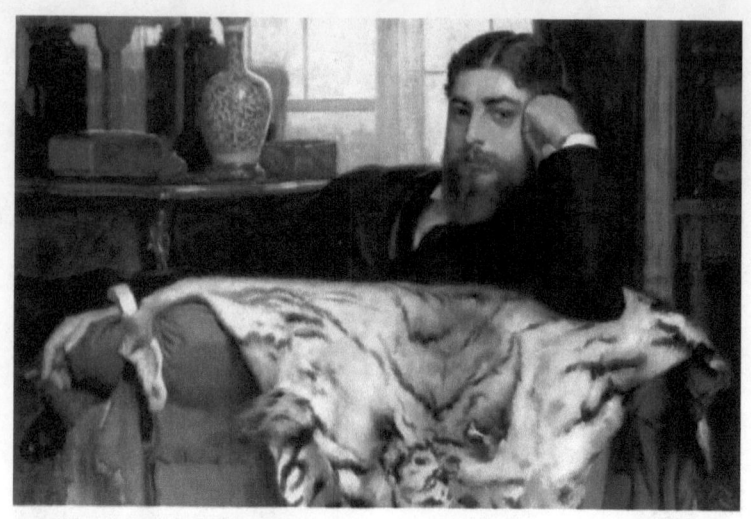

Algeron Moses Marsden
1877, oil on canvas

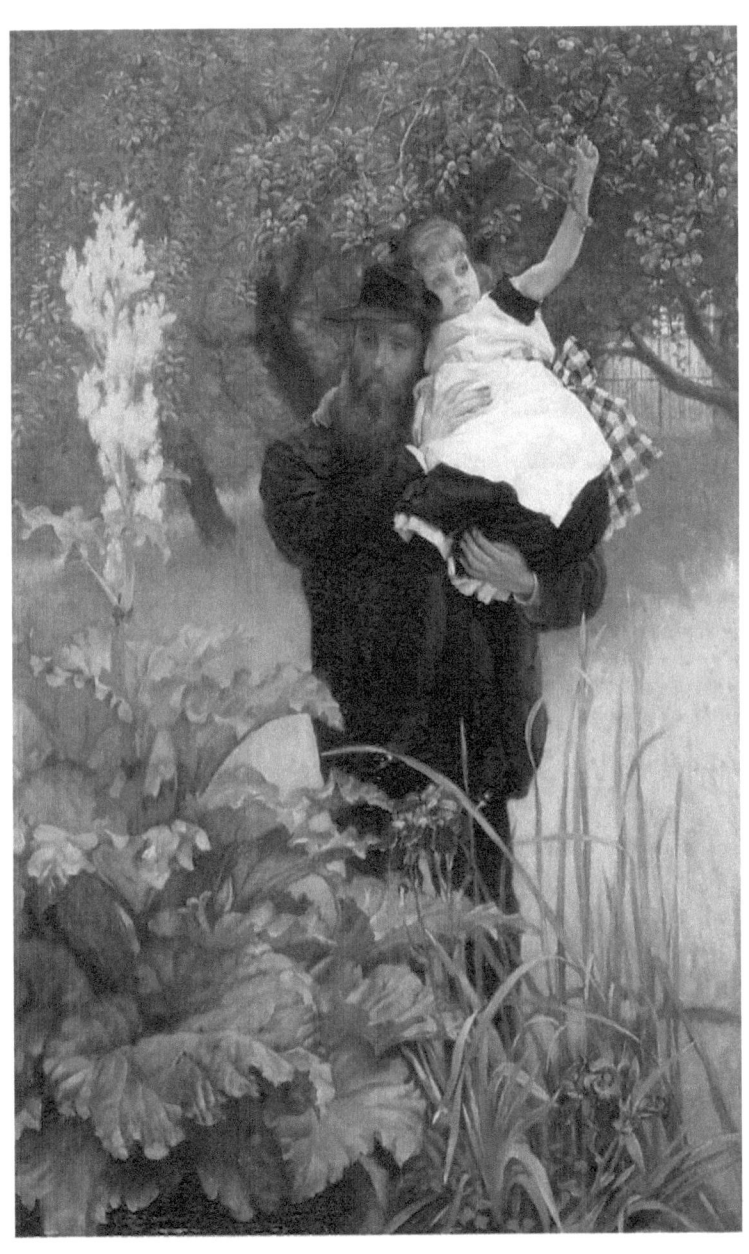

The Widower
1877, oil on canvas

Though not without a overemotional quality, this atypical work by the French painter James Tissot bespeaks an essential sincerity. The identity of the father clinging so sulkily to his child is not known. They may simply have been models. The setting, however, can be identified as the garden of Tissot's London residence in St John's Wood, a property that later passed to his colleague, the 'olympian' painter Alma-Tadema. 'The widower' has the moralising overtones of a Victorian problem picture, and it may be to the English taste for such images that Tissot was deliberately appealing. His liaison with a divorcee - a woman he frequently painted and clearly adored - placed him beyond the pale of conventional society, and beyond its patronage. It is almost tempting to see Tissot himself as the widower of the title, a man unhappily denied his mate. Technically, the work is an exercise in painterly probity: Tissot's rendering of vegetation, fabric and flesh is impressive.

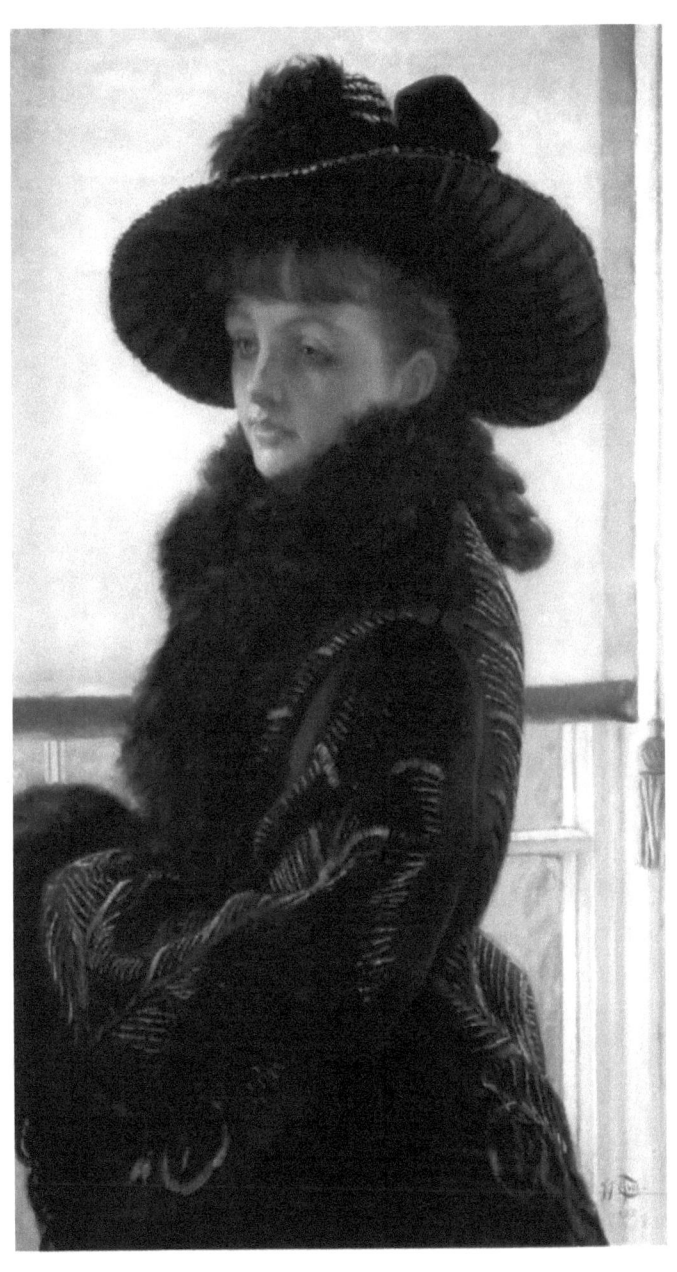

Mavourneen (Portrait of Kathleen Newton)
1877, oil on canvas

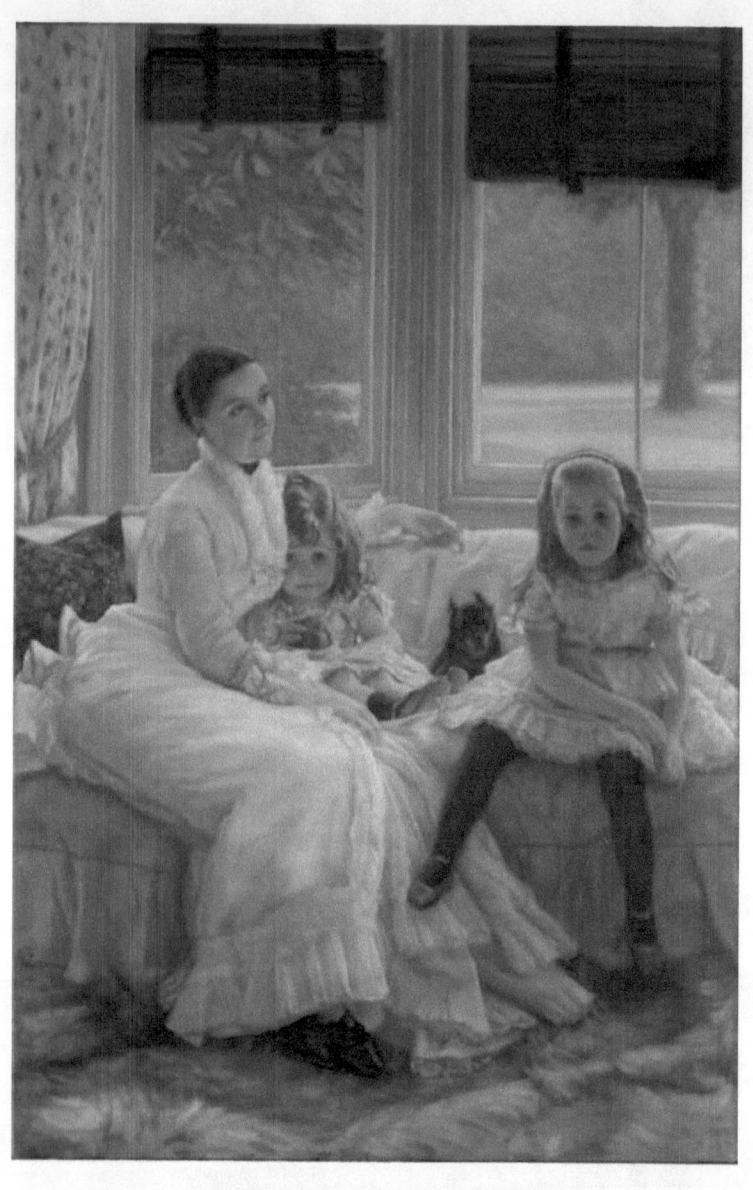

Portrait of Mrs Catherine Smith Gill and two of her
children
1877, oil on canvas

The French painter, printmaker and enamellist Jacques Tissot moved to England to escape punishment for his participation in the Paris Commune which collapsed in 1871. Tissot stayed in England for ten years and became extremely successful as a portrait painter of wealthy people, in particular fashionable ladies.

Chapple Gill, who was a senior partner in a Liverpool firm of cotton brokers commissioned Tissot to paint a portrait of his wife Catherine, their two year old son Robert and their six year old daughter Helen at their house in Woolton, Liverpool.

The care and affection with which Tissot painted Mrs Gill and captured in her face the concept of motherhood may reflect the painter's love for the Irish divorcee, Mrs Kathleen Newton. She and her two children became Tissot's favourite subject matter from 1875 until her death in 1882. The quick brushwork in the leaves of the trees, the furniture and the dress of Mrs Gill reveal the impressionist manner of Tissot who however declined an invitation by Degas in 1874 to exhibit with the Impressionists.

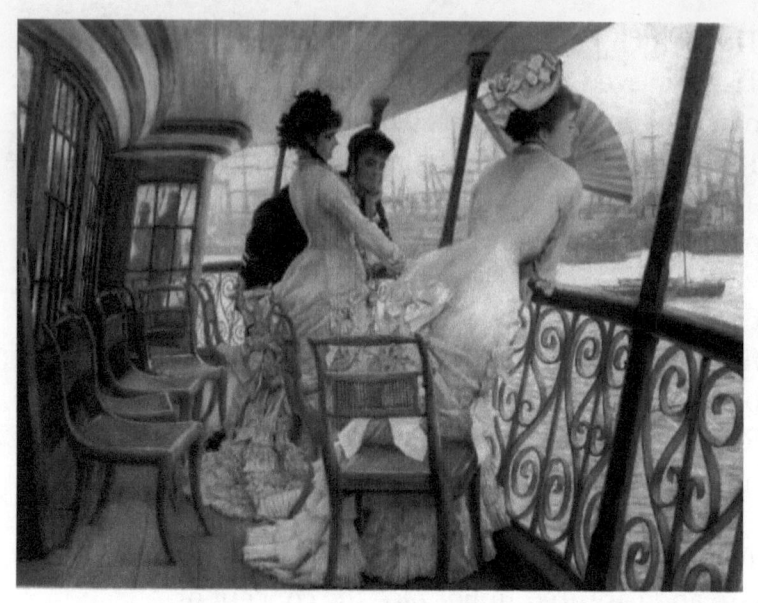

Remembrance Ball on Board
1877, oil on canvas

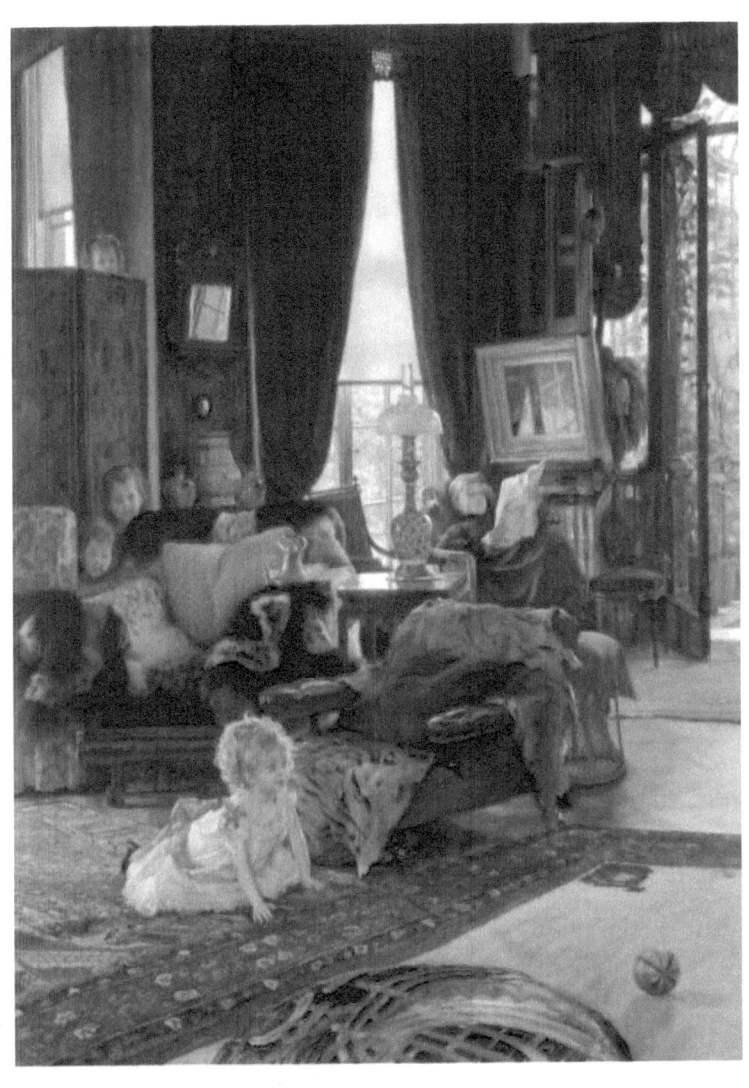

Hide and Seek
1877, oil on canvas

n early 1874 Degas wrote, "Look here, my dear Tissot. . . you positively must exhibit at the Boulevard [in the first impressionist exhibition]. . . Exhibit. Be of your country and with your friends." Degas and Tissot, who met as students during the late 1850s, stayed in close communication even after Tissot fled to London in 1871 to avoid punishment for activities in the abortive Commune. Arguing that the benefits of declaring his allegiance to French art outweighed the potential harm it might cause among Tissot's London audience, Degas urged Tissot to show with the impressionists and thereby affirm his ties to France and more particularly to Degas and realism.

Although he chose not to accept the invitation, Tissot like Degas worked in a realist vein. Hide and Seek depicts a modern, opulently cluttered Victorian room, Tissot's studio. After Kathleen Newton entered his home in about 1876, Tissot focused almost exclusively on intimate, anecdotal descriptions of the activities of the secluded suburban household, depicting an idyllic world tinged by a melancholy awareness of the illness that would lead to her death in 1882. The artist's companion reads in a corner as her nieces and daughter amuse themselves. The artist injected an atmosphere of unease into this tranquil scene by comparing the three lively faces peering toward the infant in the foreground at the left with an ashen Japanese mask hanging near Mrs. Newton in the entry to the conservatory.

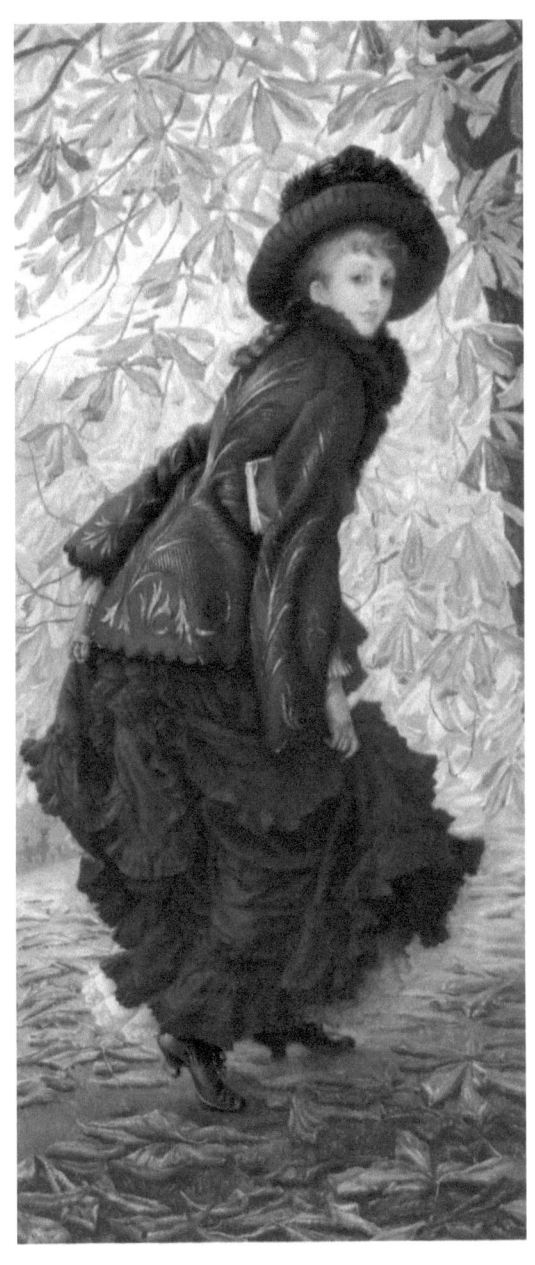

October
1878, oil on canvas

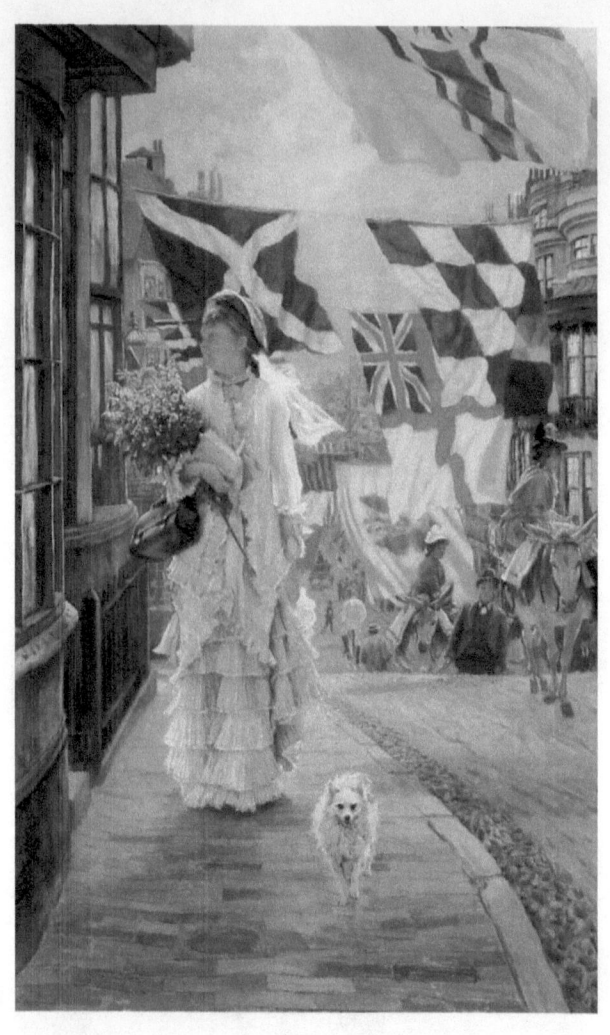

A Fete Day at Brighton (Naval flags of various
European nations seen In background)
1878, oil on canvas

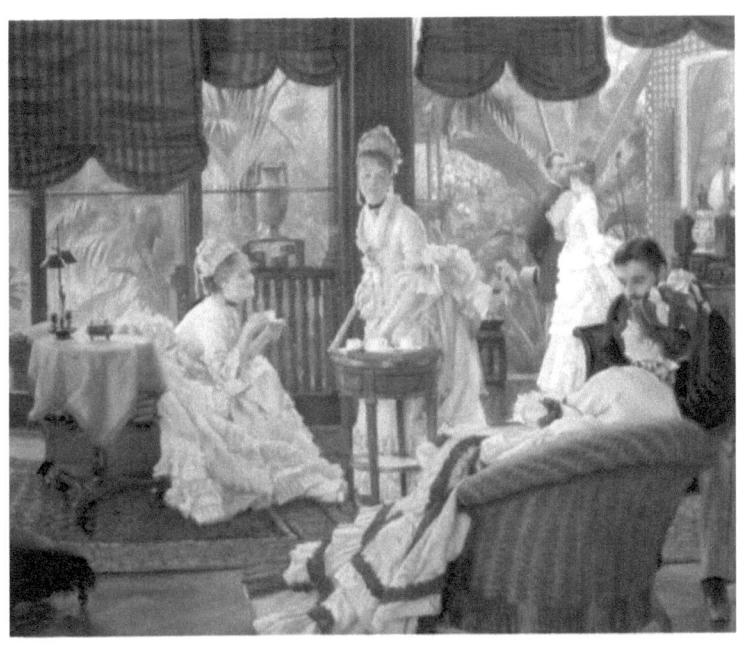

In the Conservatory
1878, oil on canvas

Although the artist's given title for this painting is lost, it is clearly a comedy of manners — Tissot's favorite English narrative subject — involving twin sisters, their mother, a potential suitor, and a further pair of figures whose identities are less obvious. Recent scholarship suggests that Tissot may have drawn on a literary source for this work, George John Whyte-Melville's popular novel "M. or N." (1869).

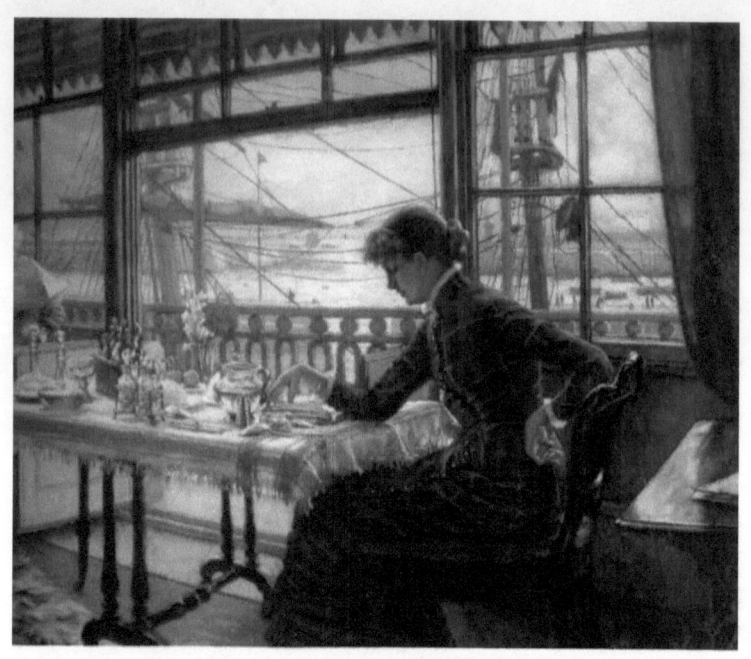

Room Overlooking the Harbour
1878, oil on canvas

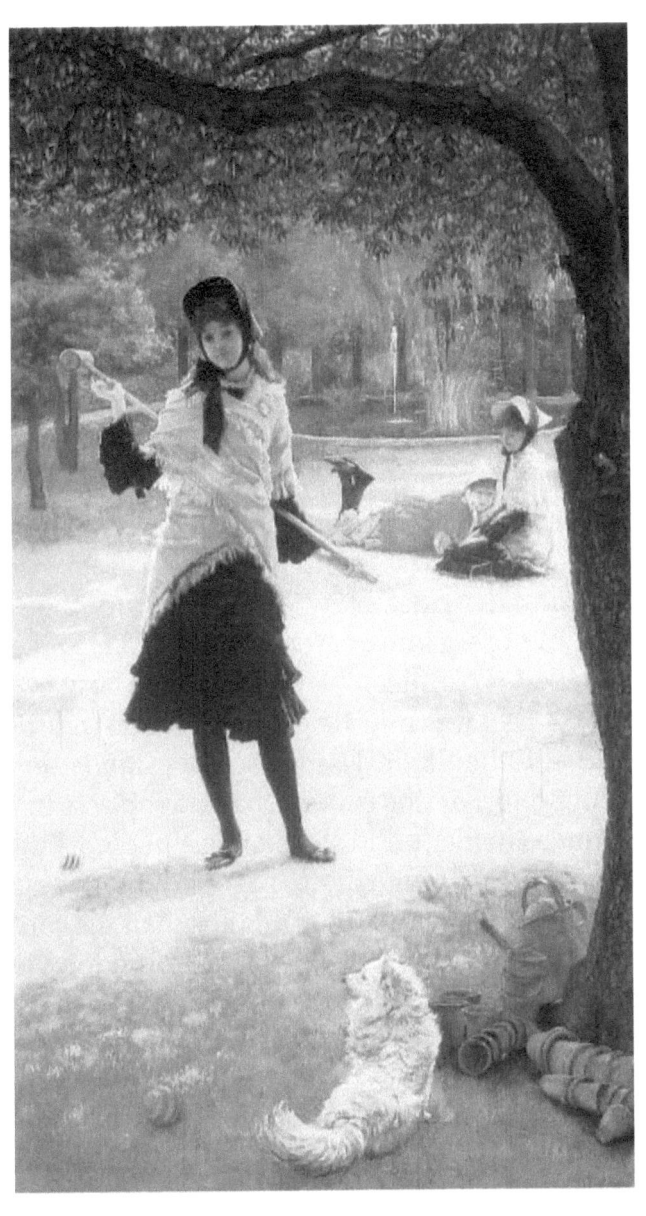

Croquet
1878, oil on canvas

This painting clearly demonstrates the three levels of fore, middle, and background. Tissot has made items in the background appear to be further away than items in the foreground by making colours fade as they move into the background. He has also created depth by making figures in the background smaller and higher than those in the foreground. In the foreground of this painting sits a small white dog, a croquet ball and some other items at the base of a tree, quite close to the bottom of the painting. These items are at the front of the painting and grab the viewer's attention. The foreground is 'inviting' the viewer into the scene, but it does not show us what action is taking place. The main subject is in the middle ground holding a croquet mallet behind her back. Now we can identify the action in this painting: a game of croquet. We can also identify the woman: it is Kathleen Newton. Notice how brightly lit the grass is in this middle ground section in order to draw our attention to it. Tissot's subject stands several inches higher up on the canvas than the objects in the foreground. Further off in the distance behind Kathleen are two young girls who are lounging in the grass. These subjects are placed even higher than the middle ground subject, to show their distance from the viewer. The trees seem to fade in colour and detail as they recede into the background. This area is also in shade, drawing our attention to the brightly lit middle ground.

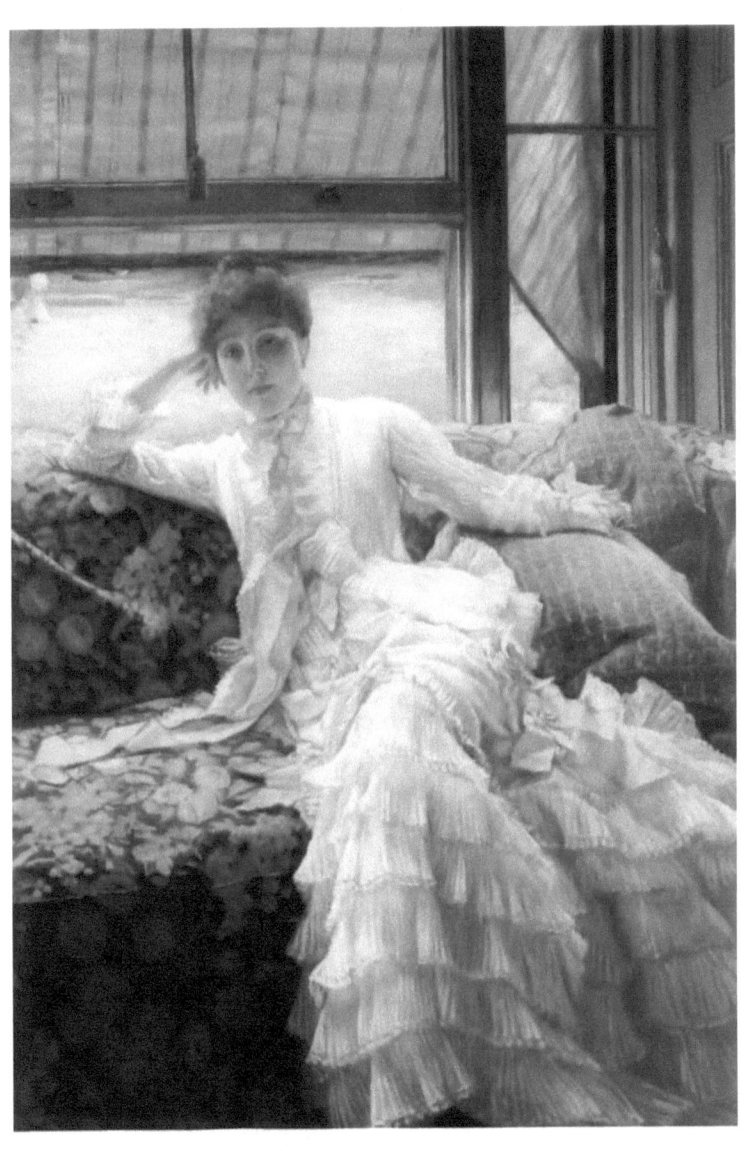

Spring
1878, oil on canvas

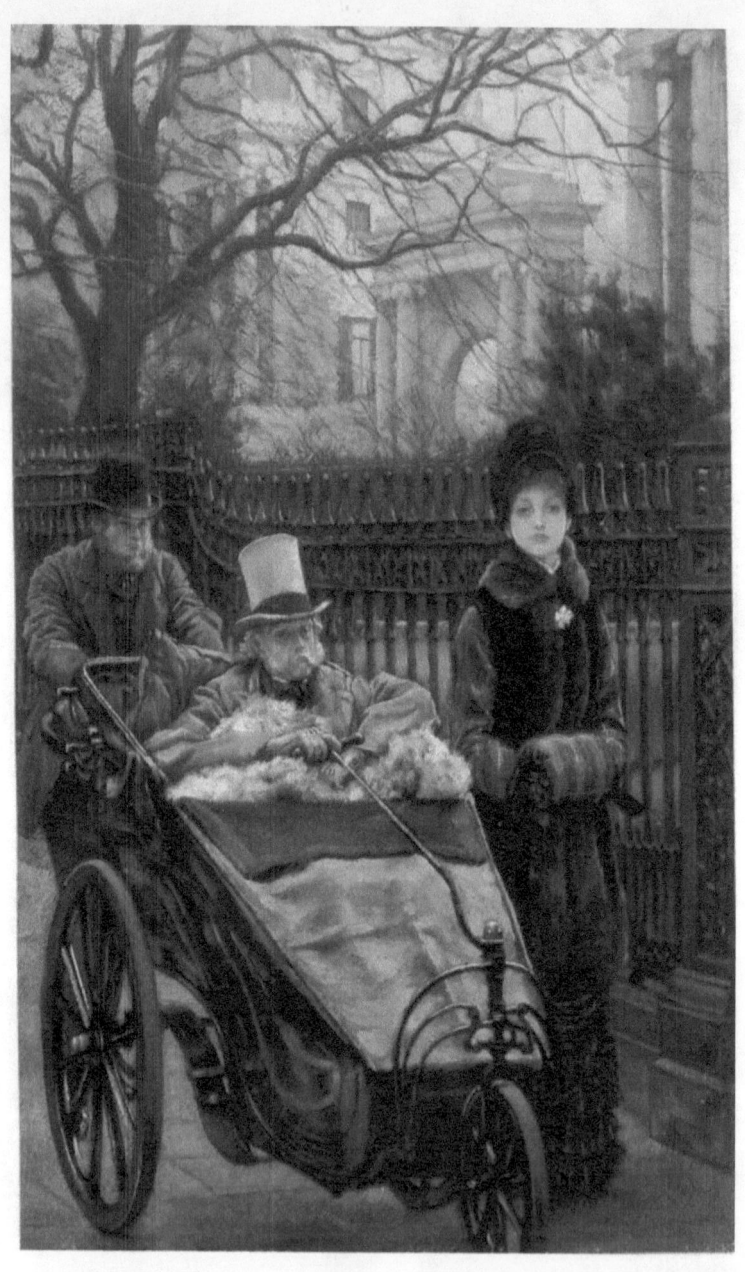

The Warrior's Daughter or the Convalescent
1878, oil on canvas

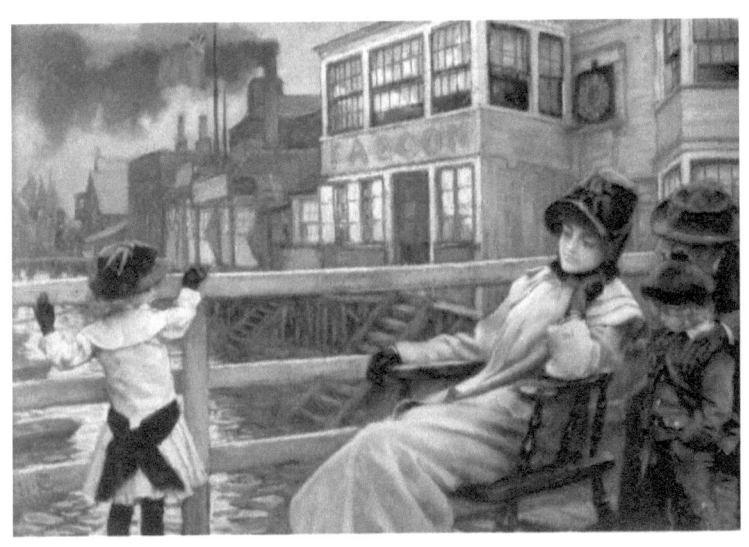

Waiting for the Ferry
1878, oil on canvas

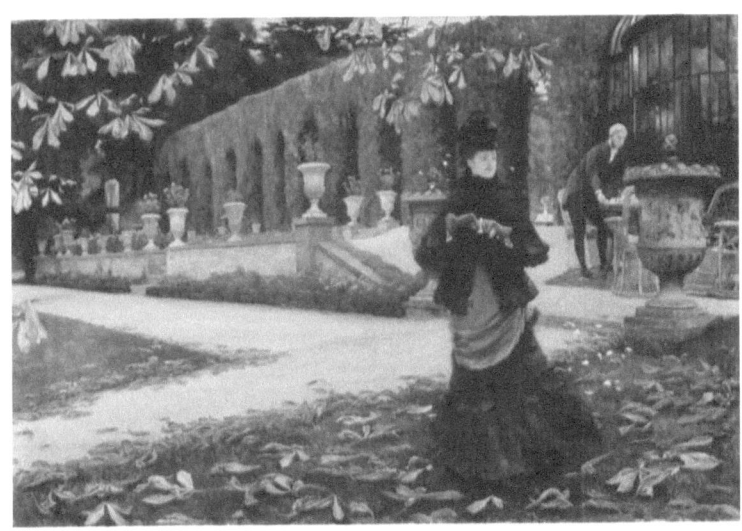

The Letter,
1878, oil on canvas

Jacques-Joseph Tissot, known as James, resided in London from 1871 until 1882. The scenes of leisure life and fashion he painted there brought him remarkable financial success: Edgar Degas was astounded to learn that in 1873 Tissot had received 900 pounds for a painting. The appeal of Tissot's work lies in its lavish detail and a choice of subject inspired by contemporary British society. Here every fold and ruffle of the model's clothing, down to the raised seam of her leather gloves, is rendered with vivid and exacting precision. The setting for "The Letter" has recently been identified as the Dutch Gardens of Holland House in London. The painting is thought to represent a falling out between Lady Holland and her adopted daughter, Marie Liechtenstein.

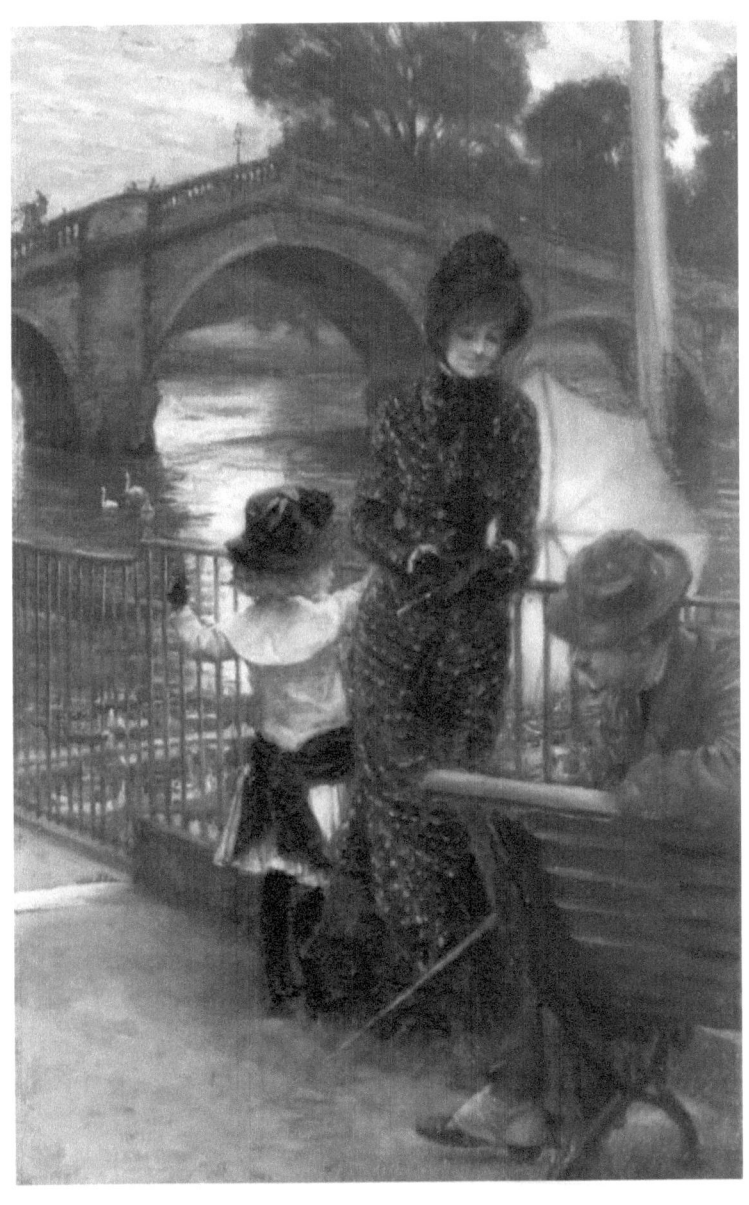

By the Thames at Richmond
1879, oil on canvas

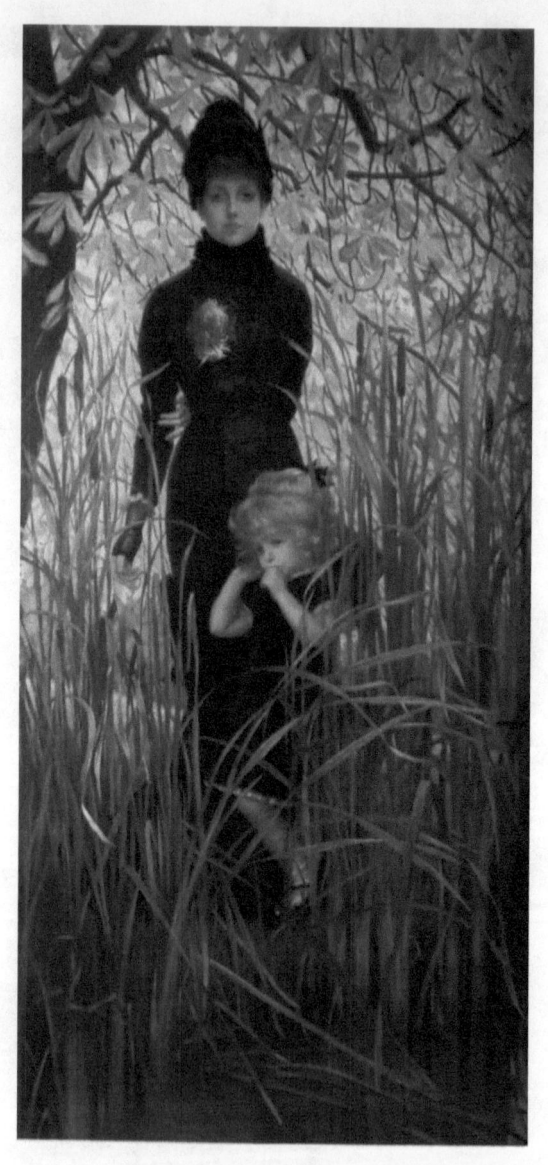

Orphan
1879, oil on canvas

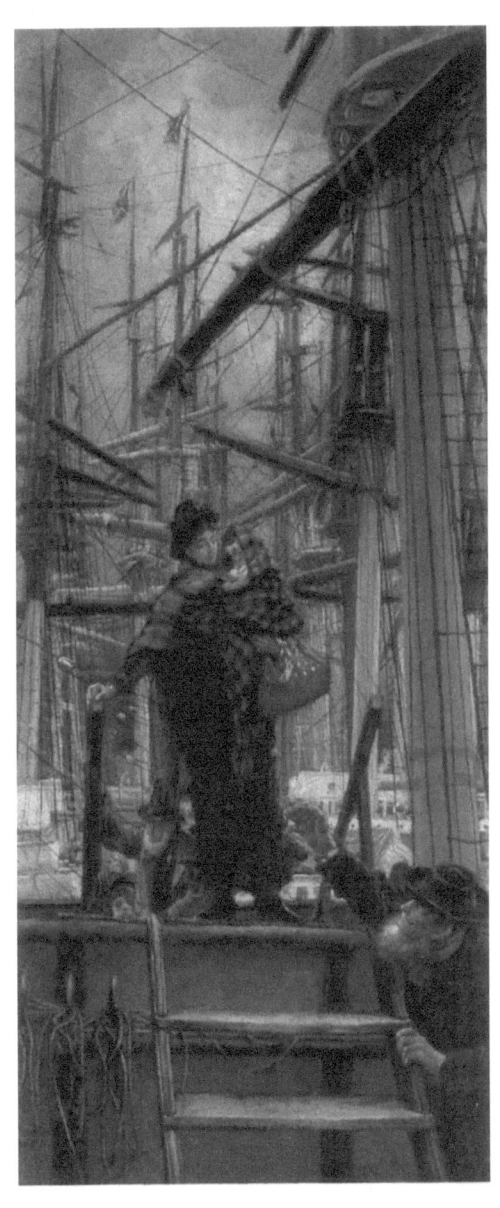

Emigrants
1879, oil on canvas

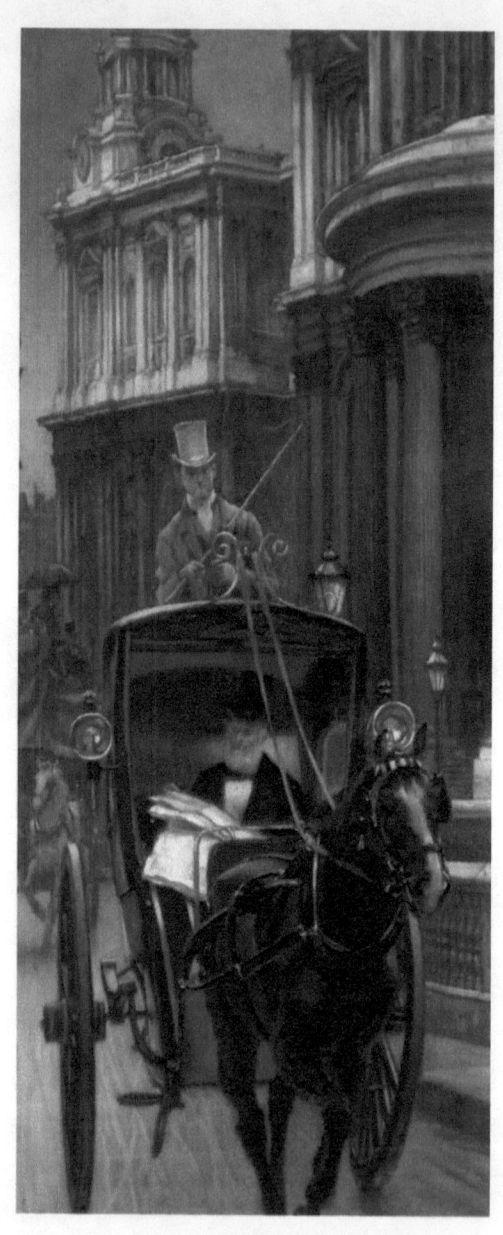

Going to Business
1879, oil on canvas

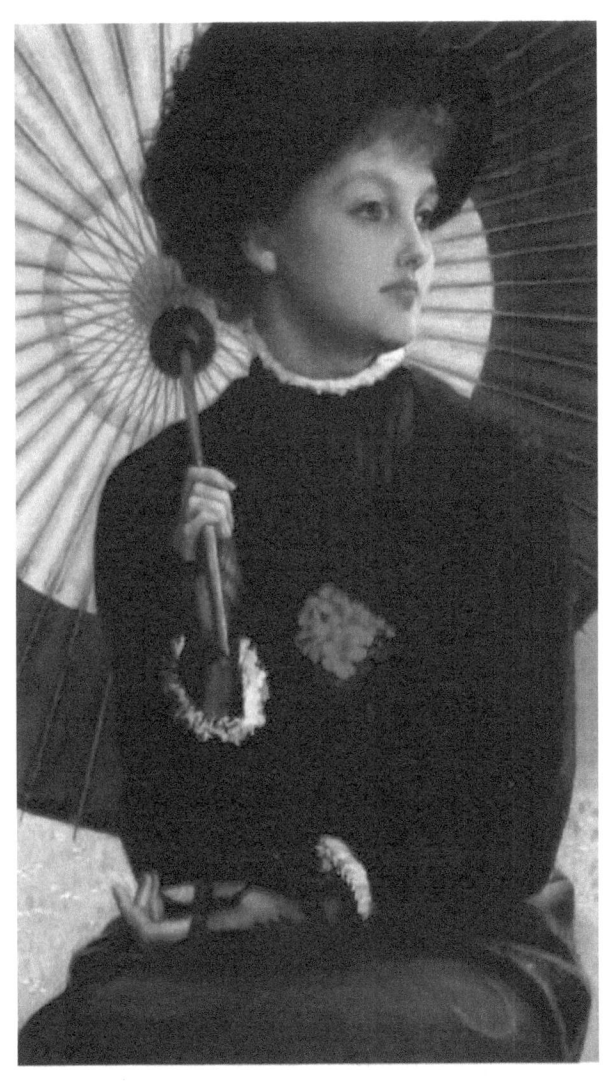

Summer (Mrs. Newton with a Parasol)
1879, oil on canvas

The sitter in Summer is Mrs Kathleen Newton, Tissot's mistress and muse, who came to live with him at his house in St John's Wood some time during 1876. She became his principal model and his work increasingly focused around their home life, until her death from tuberculosis in November 1882. The three-quarter pose enabled Tissot to show her large eyes, delicate nose and full lips to best advantage. The red of her lips is echoed in the nosegay of red flowers pinned at her breast. These are nasturtiums, a flower symbolic of 'conquest' and 'victory in battle' in the 'language of flowers' used in the past to express feelings to others - perhaps a conscious choice, as both Kathleen and Tissot were 'conquered by love'.

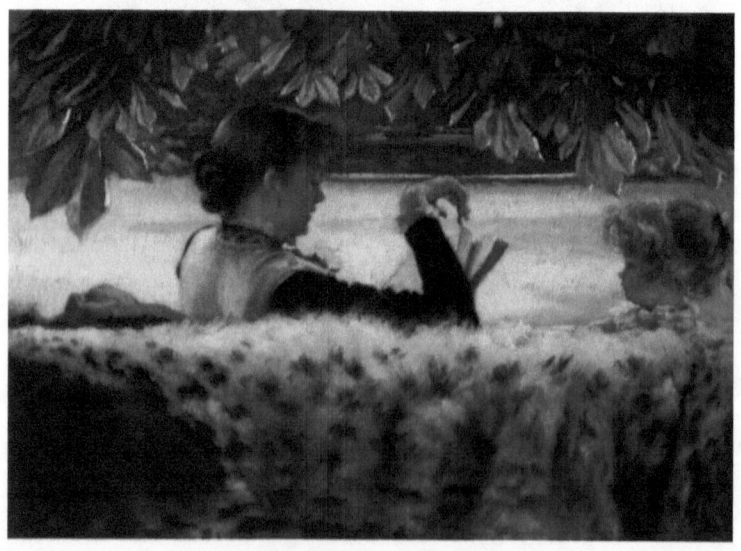

Reading a Story
1879, oil on canvas

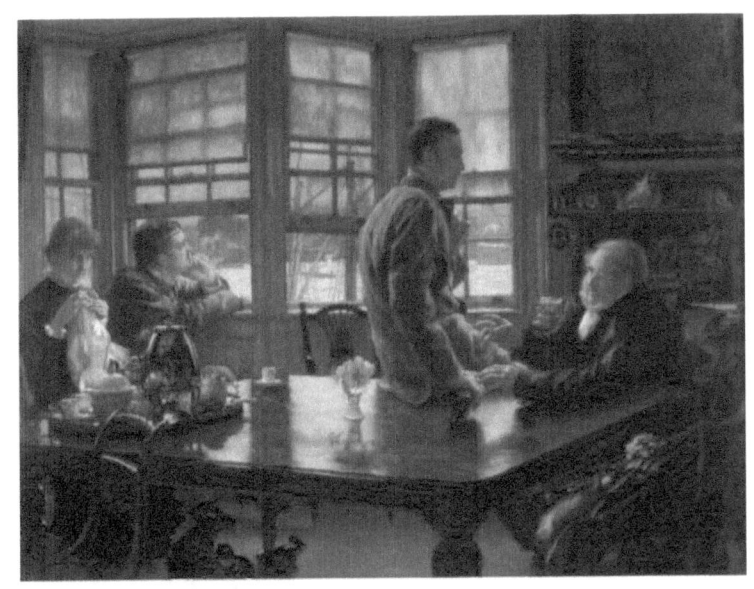

The Prodigal Son in Modern Life: The Departure
1880, oil on canvas

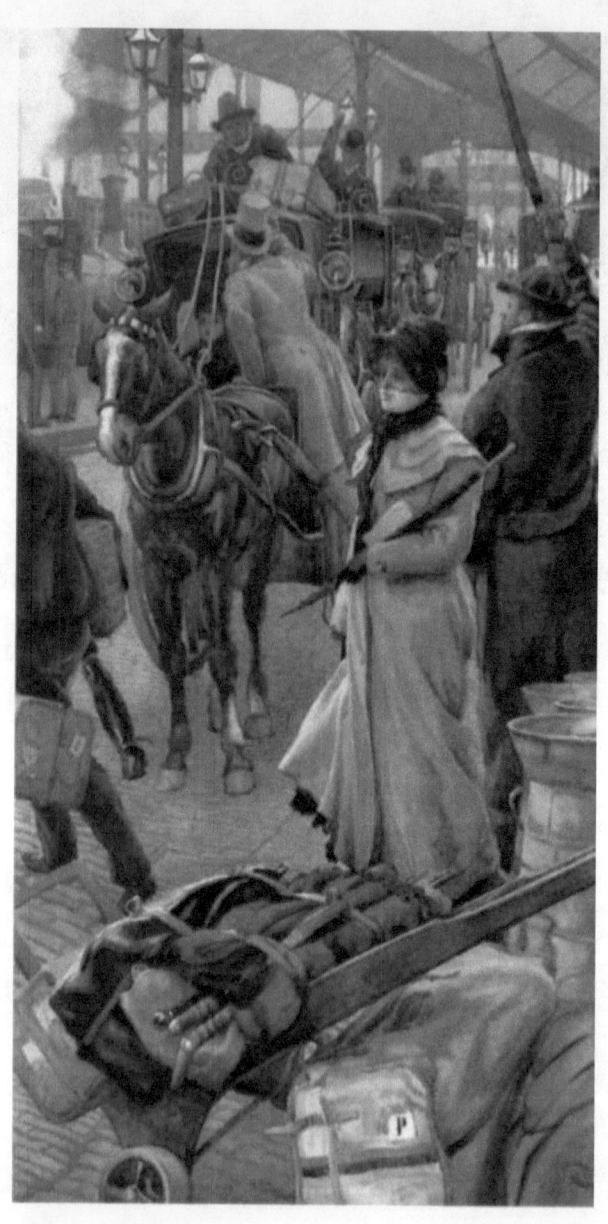

The Departure Platform, Victoria Station, 1880
Watercolor

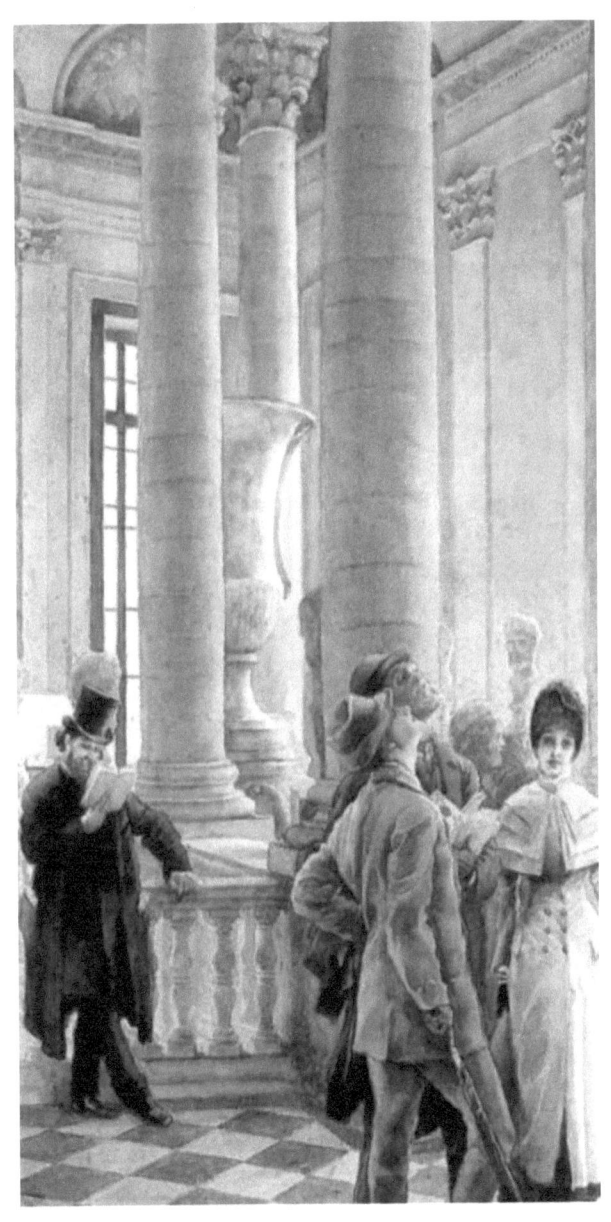

At The Louvre, 1879-1880
Watercolor

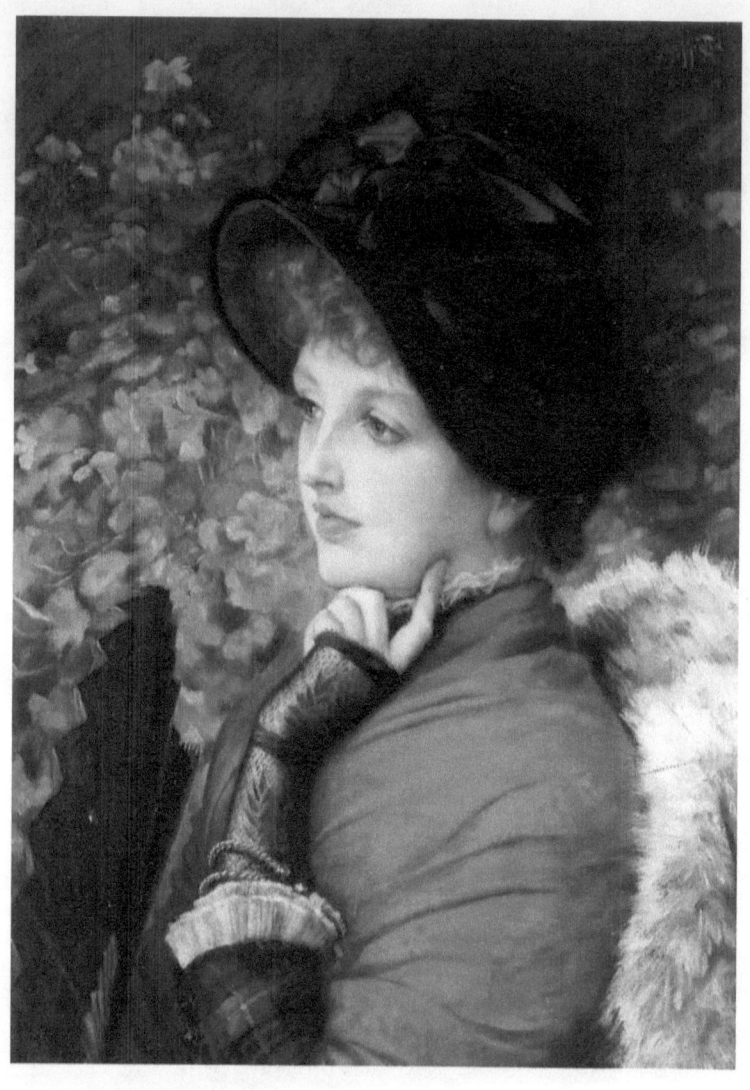

Type of Beauty: Portrait of Mrs. Kathleen Newton in a
red dress and black bonnet
1880, oil on canvas

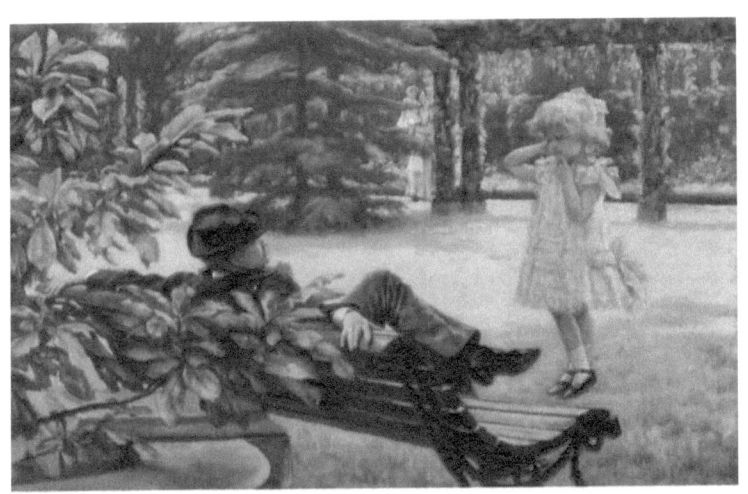

Uncle Fred
1880, oil on canvas

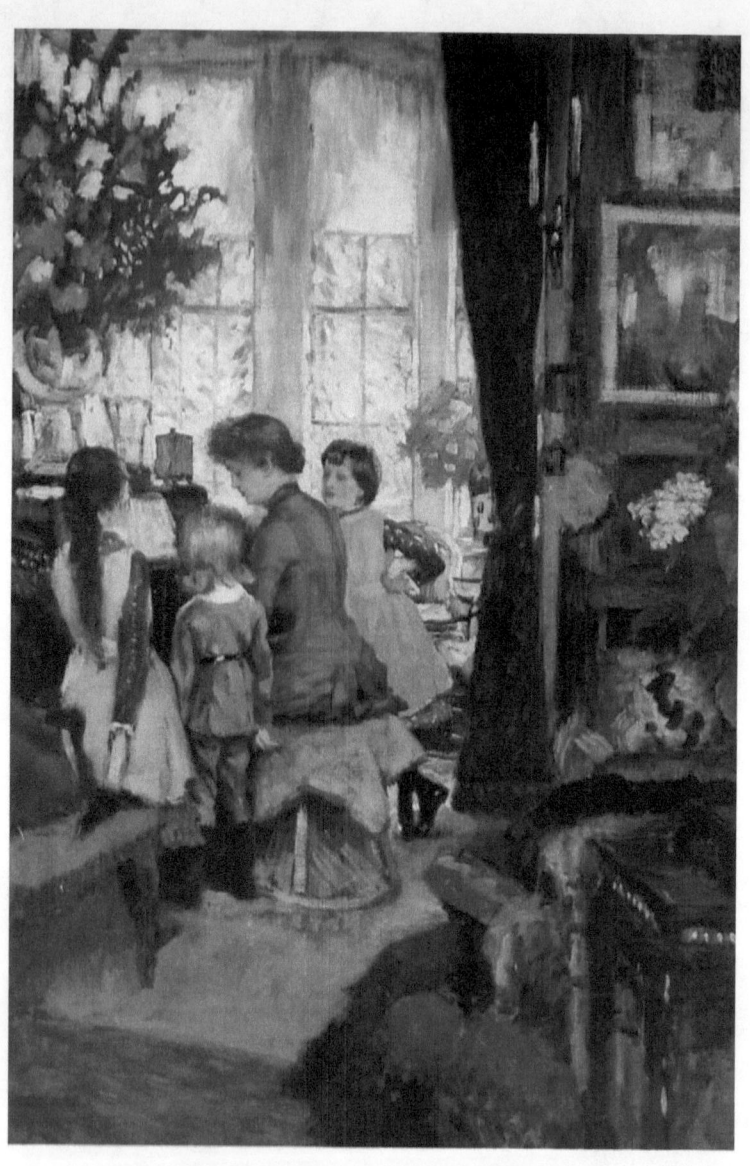

Kathleen Newton at the Piano
1881, oil on canvas

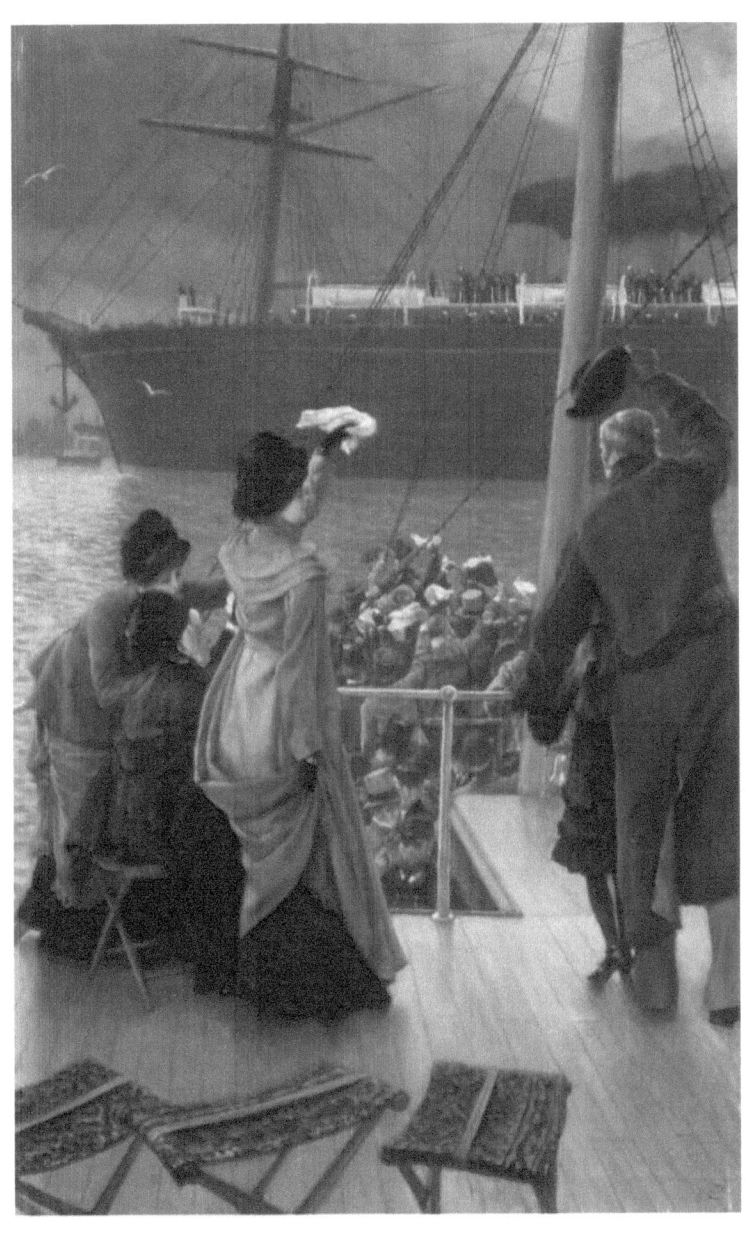

Goodbye, on the Mersey
1881, oil on canvas

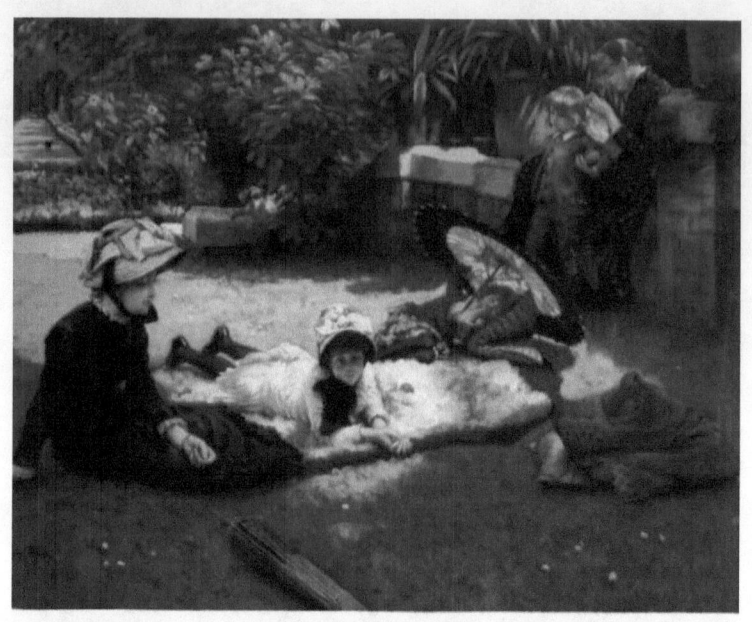

In the Sunshine
1881, oil on canvas

This group portrait includes the artist's companion,
Kathleen Newton (1854–1882), at left; her children,
Cecil George Newton (1876–1941) and Muriel Mary
Violet Newton (1871–1933); and two unidentified
figures. The setting appears to be Tissot's garden in St.
John's Wood, London.

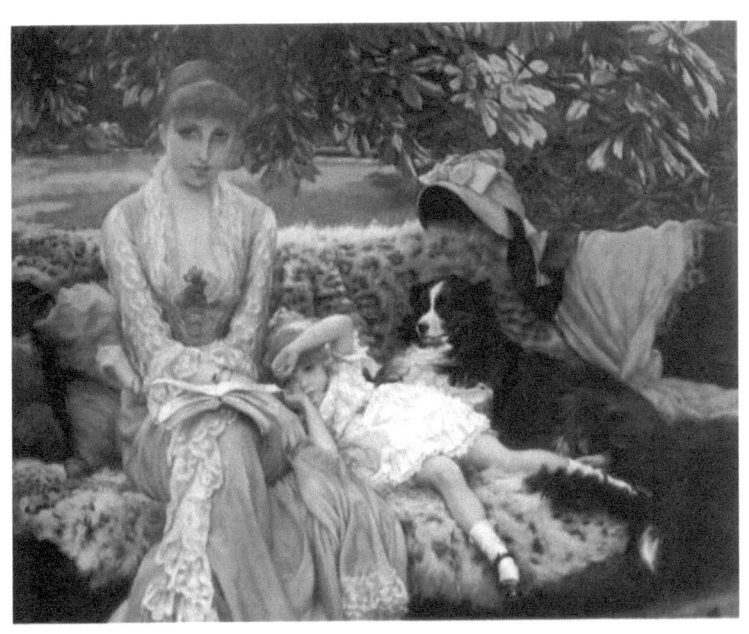

Quietn
1881, oil on canvas

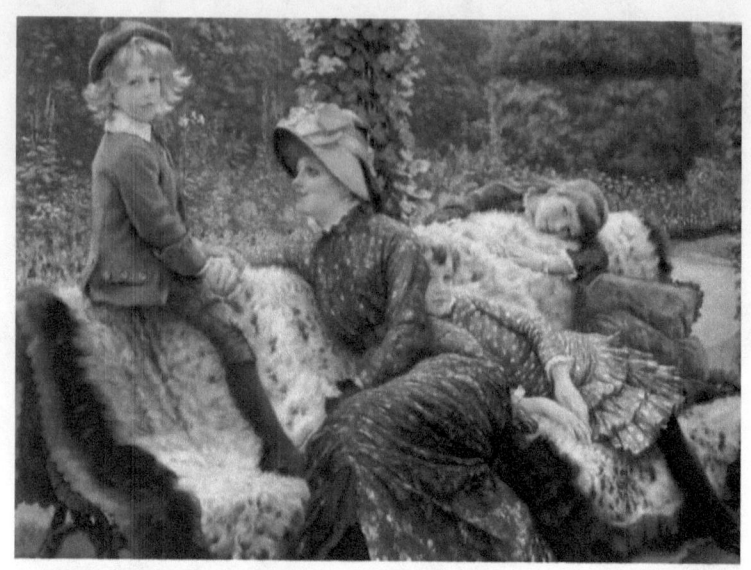

The Garden Bench
1882, oil on canvas

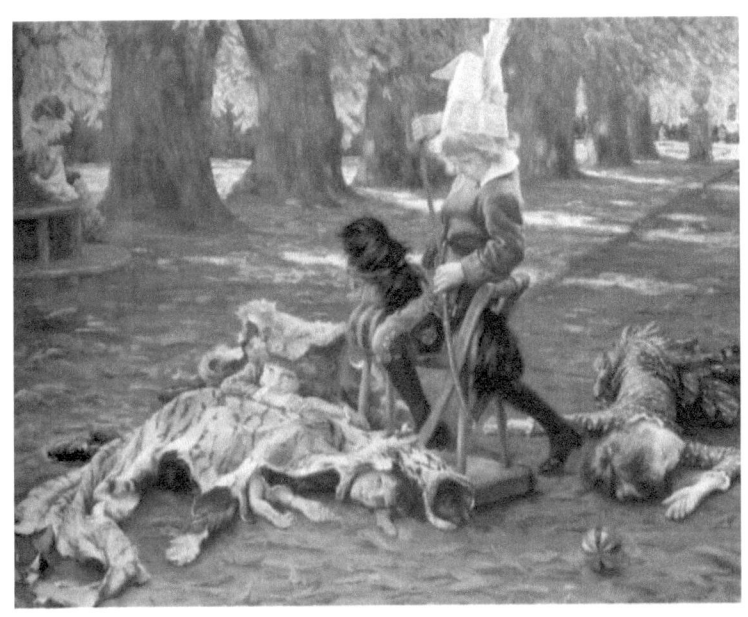

A Little Nimrod
1882, oil on canvas

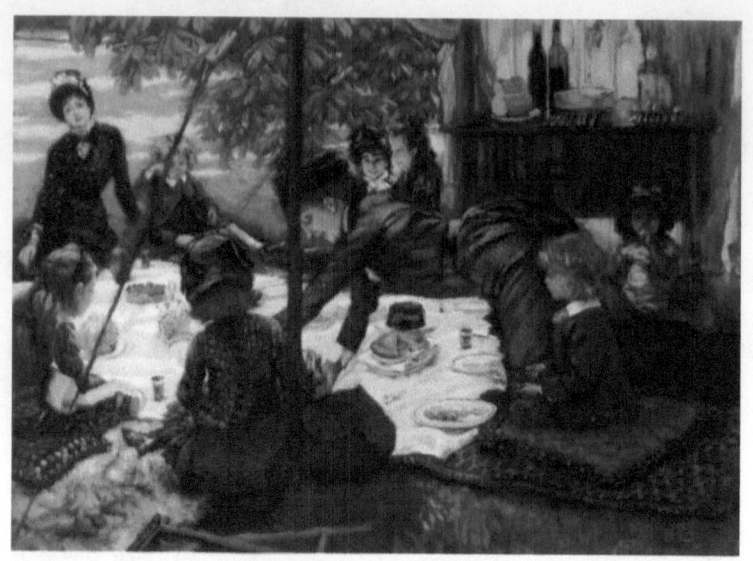

Children's Party
1882, oil on canvas

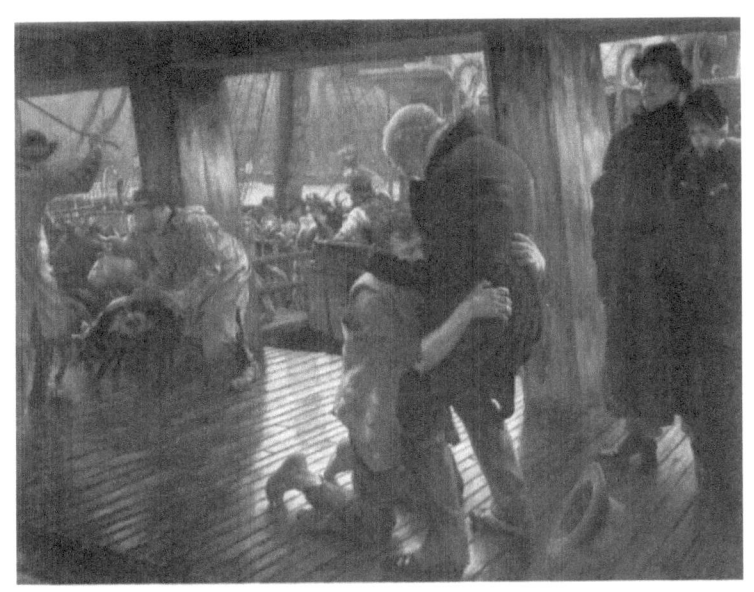

Prodigal Son, the Return
1882, oil on canvas

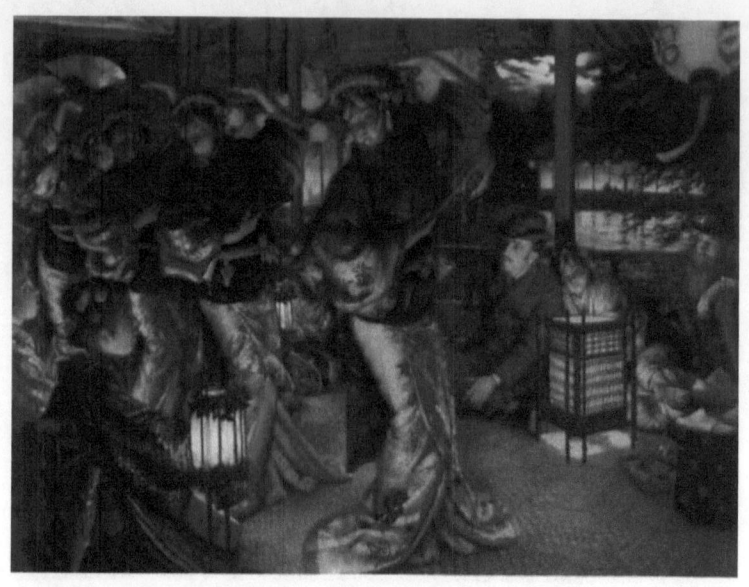

The Prodigal Son in Modern Life in Foreign Climes
1882, oil on canvas

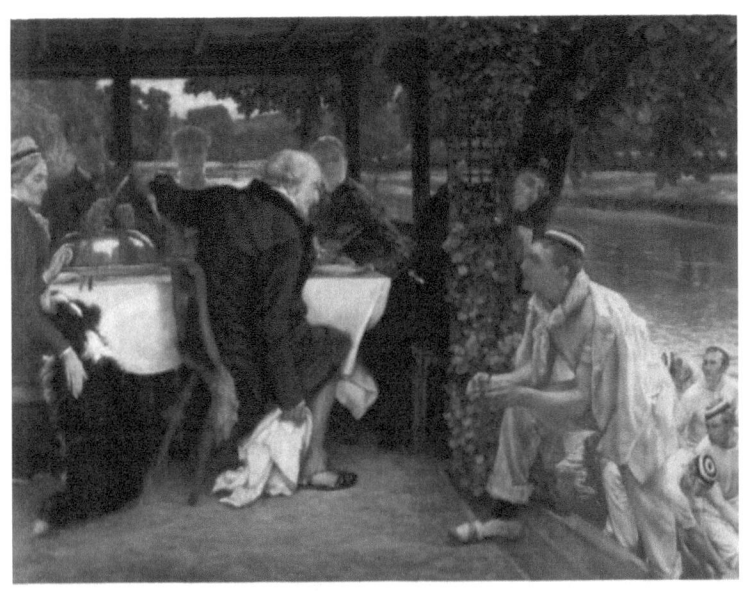

The Prodigal Son in Modern Life, the Fatted Calf
1882, oil on canvas

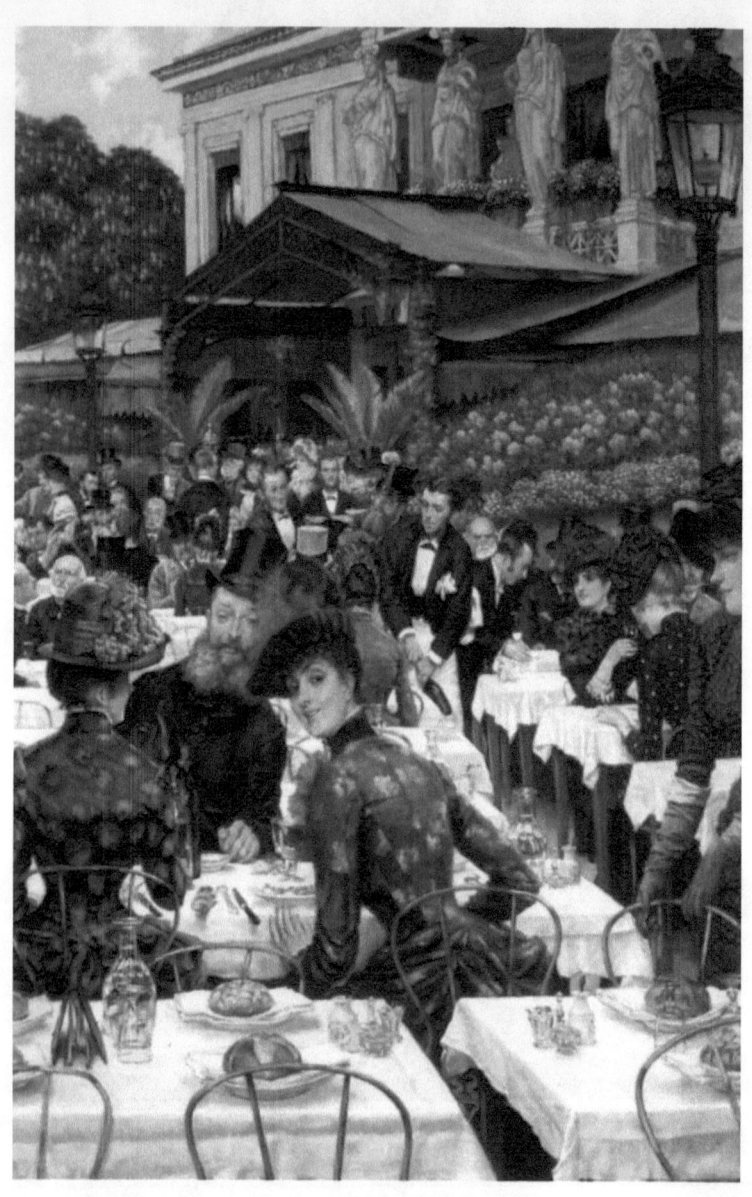

The Artist's Ladies
1885, oil on canvas

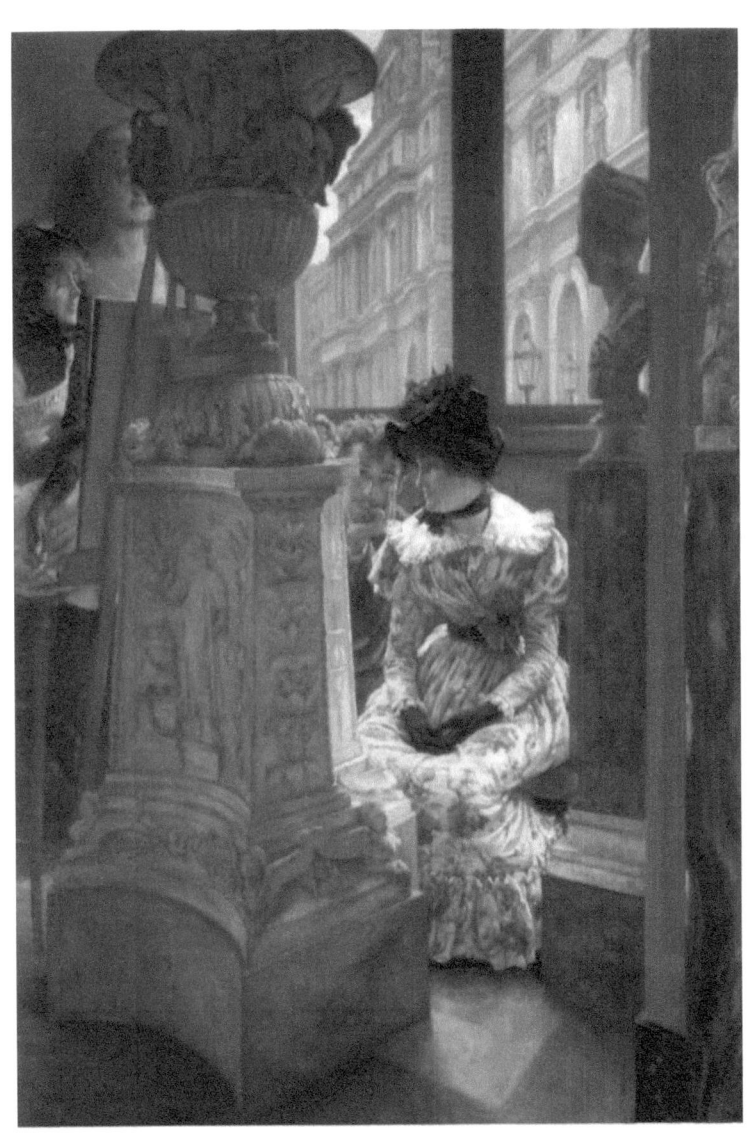

In The Louvre
1885, oil on canvas

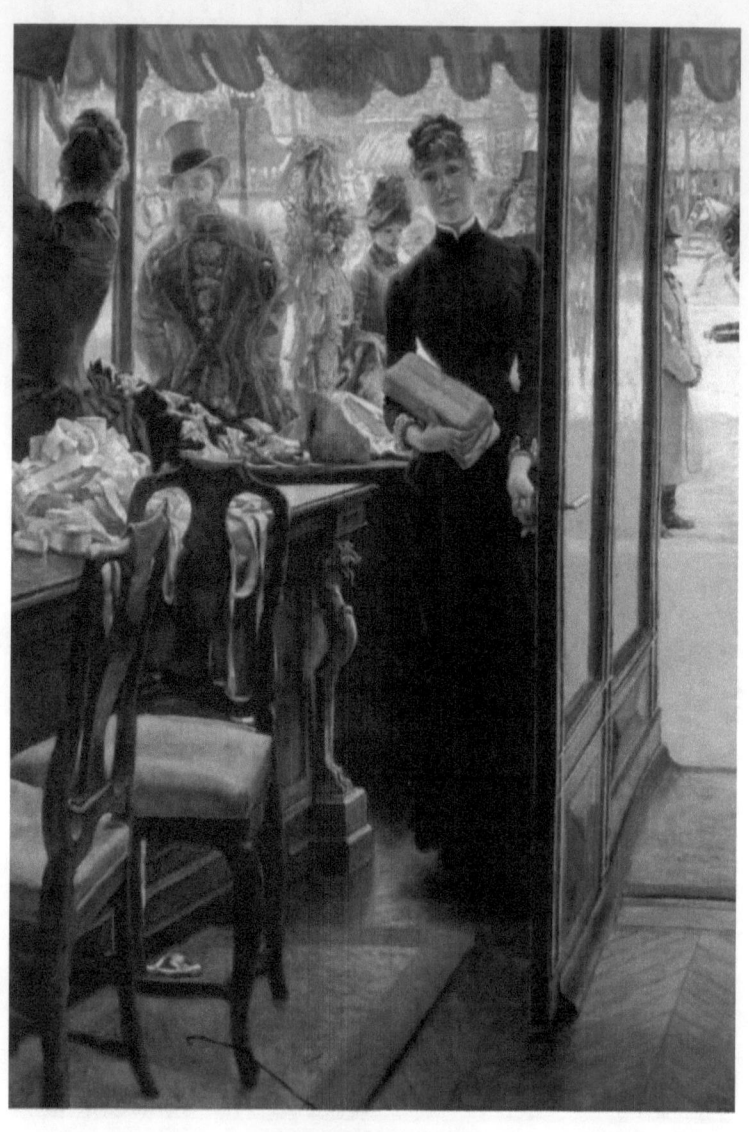

The Shop Girl
1885, oil on canvas

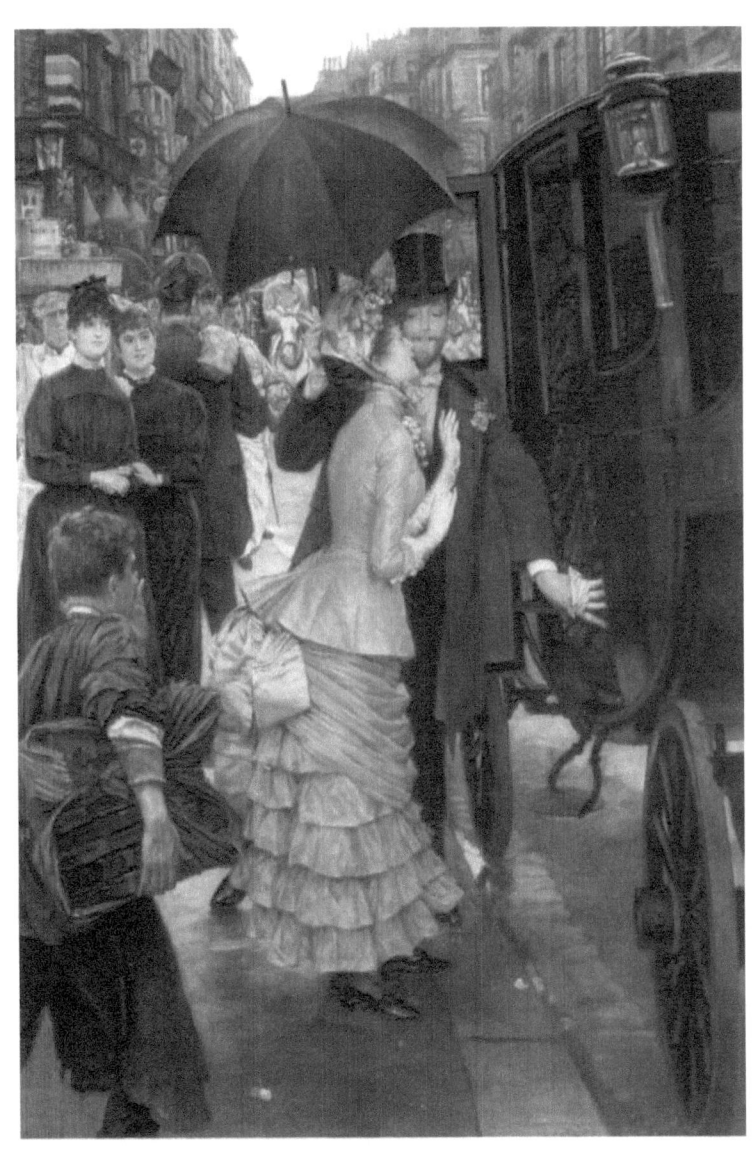

The Traveller
1885, oil on canvas

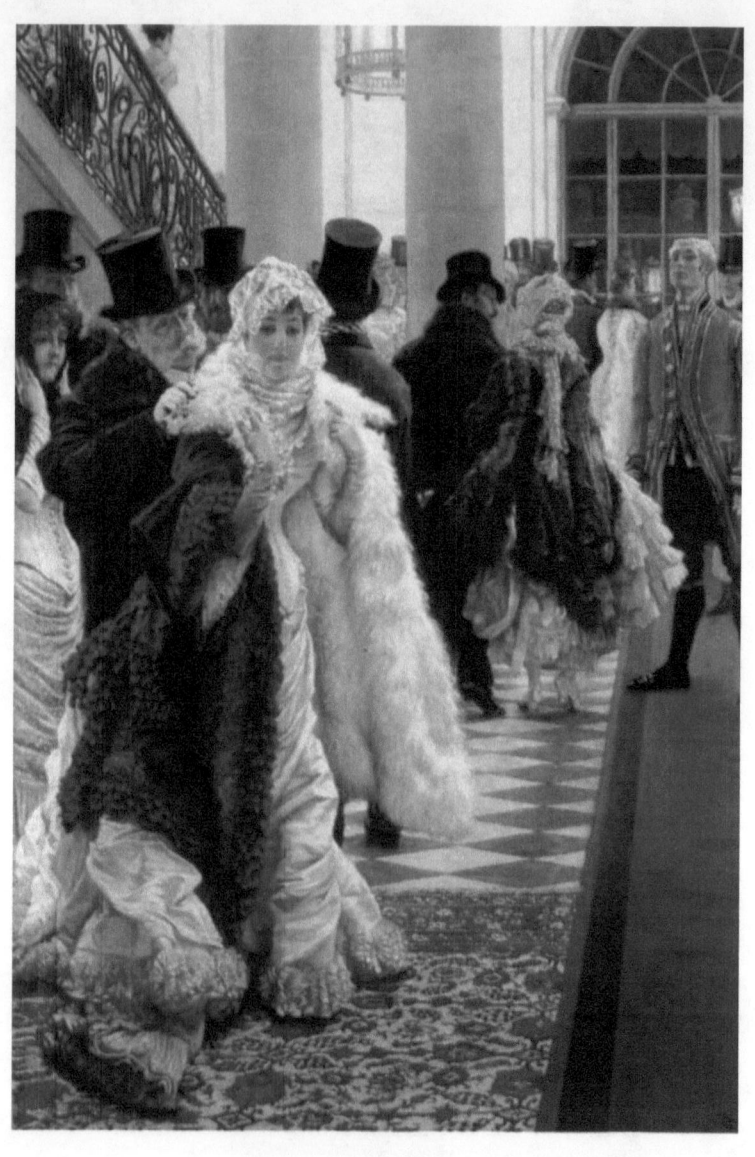

The Woman of Fashion (La Mondaine)
1885, oil on canvas

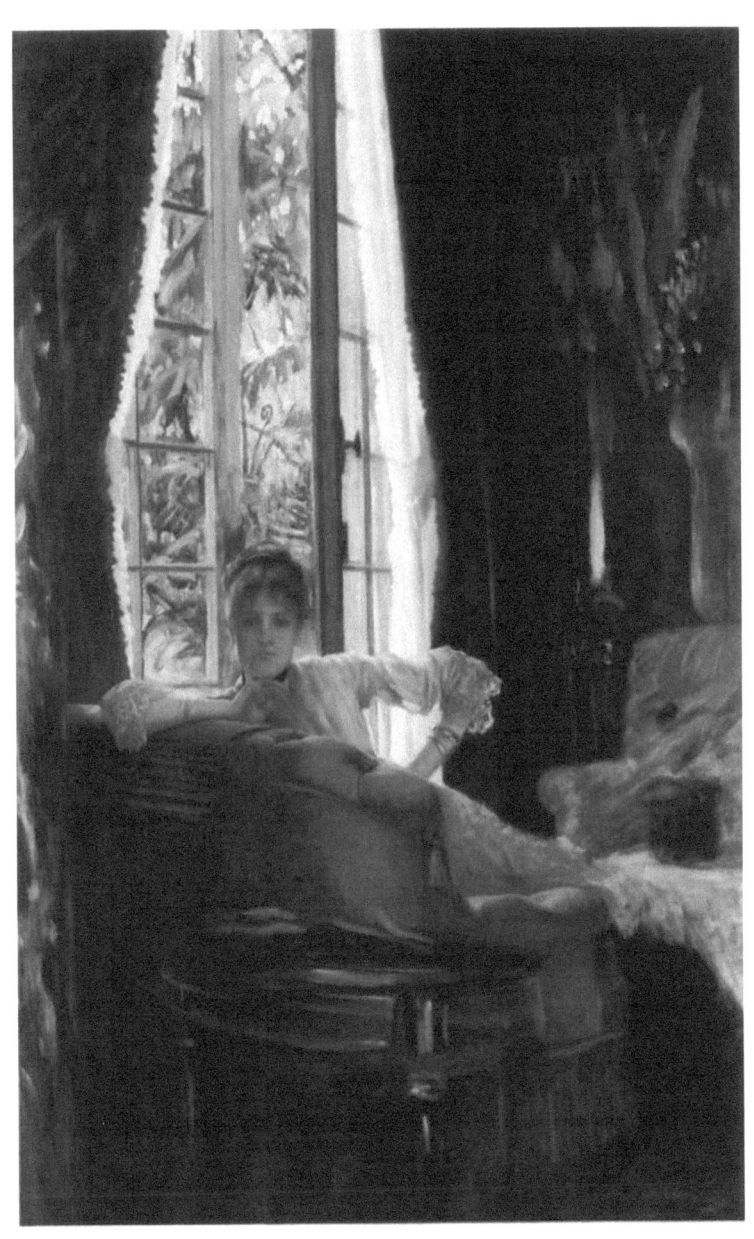

Woman in an Interior
1885, oil on canvas

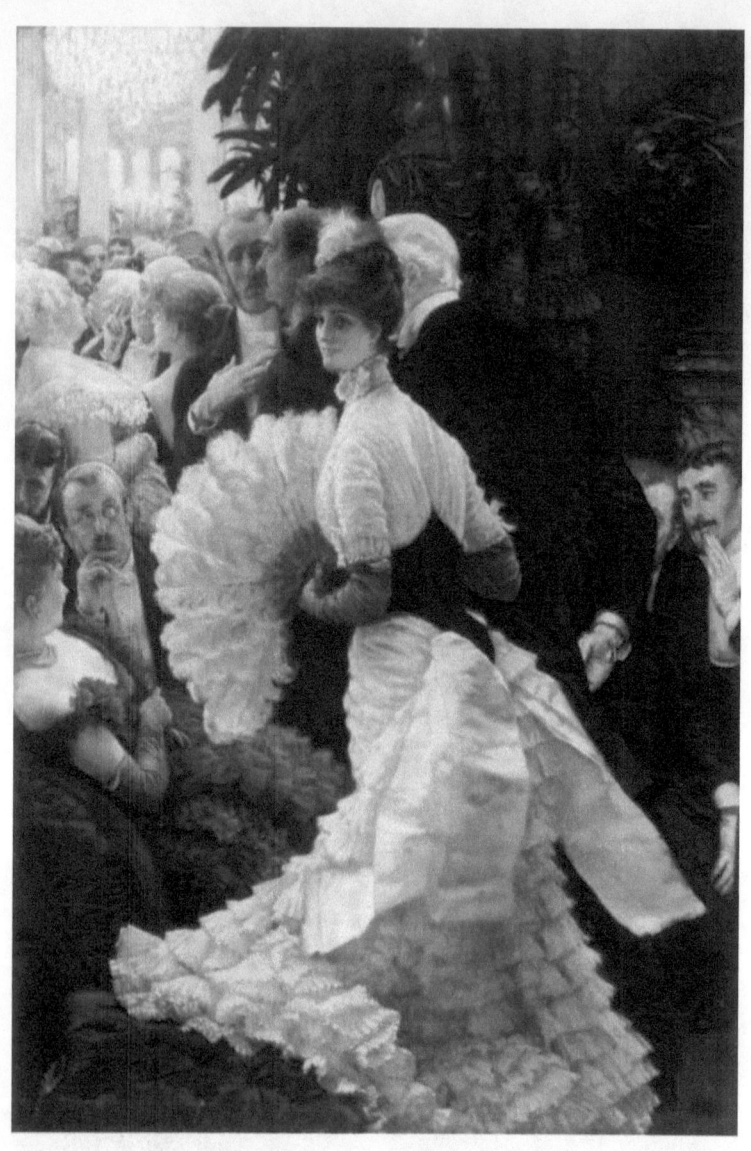

The Political Lady
1885, oil on canvas

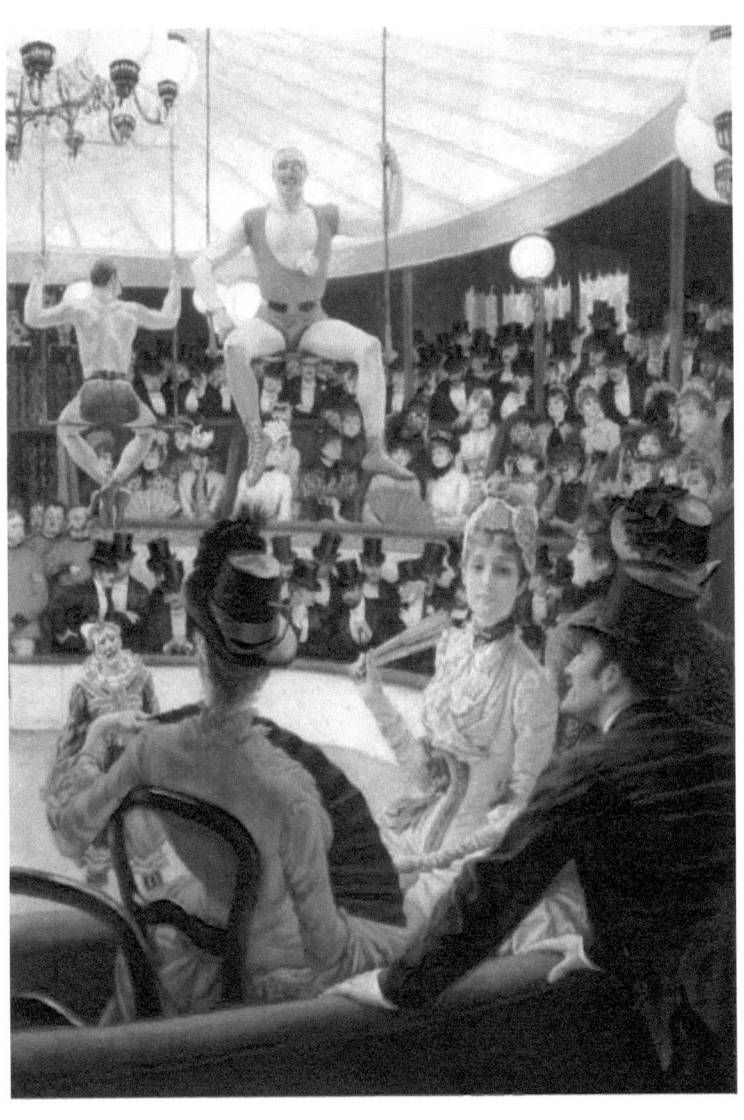

Women of Paris: The Circus Lover
1885, oil on canvas

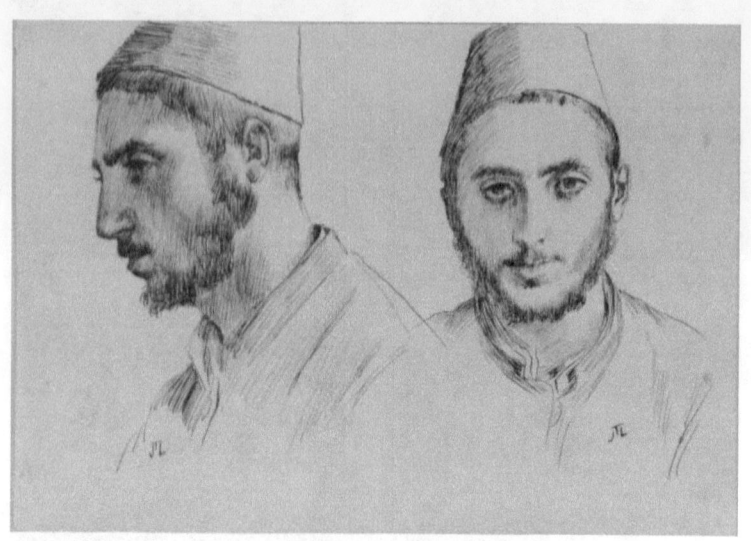

Armenians, 1886-1889
Ink

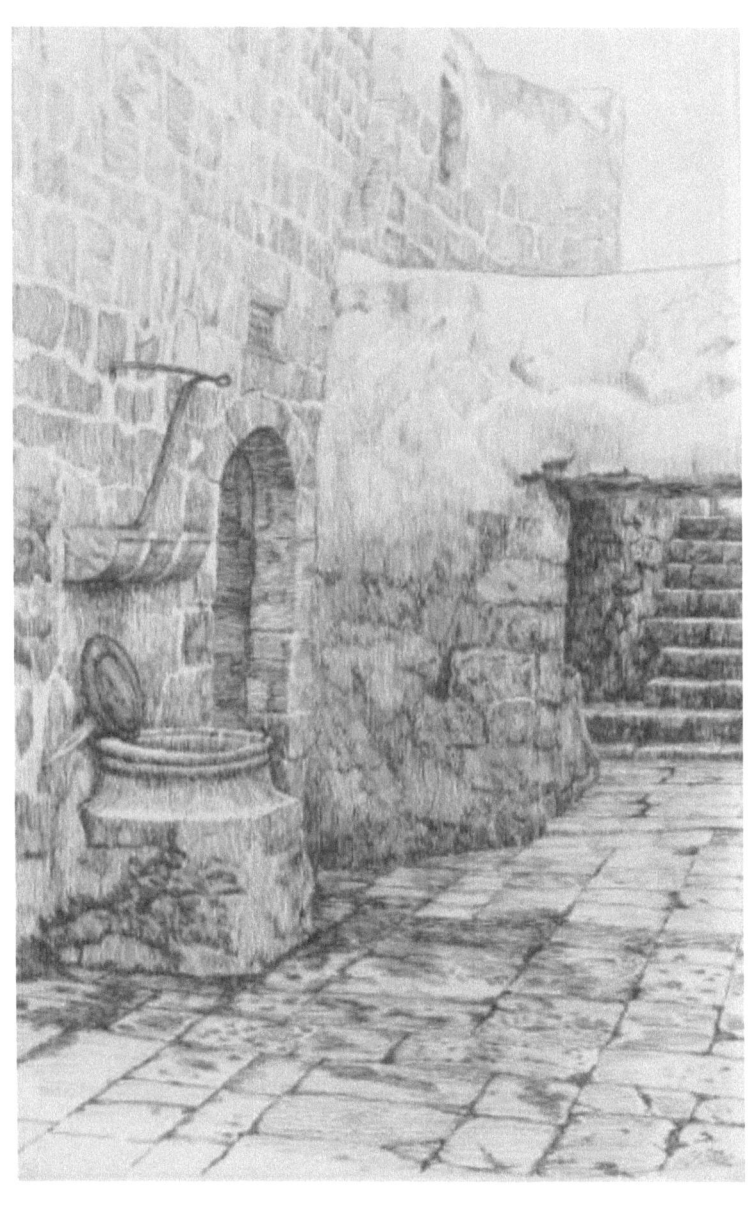

An Old Cistern, 1886-1889
Ink

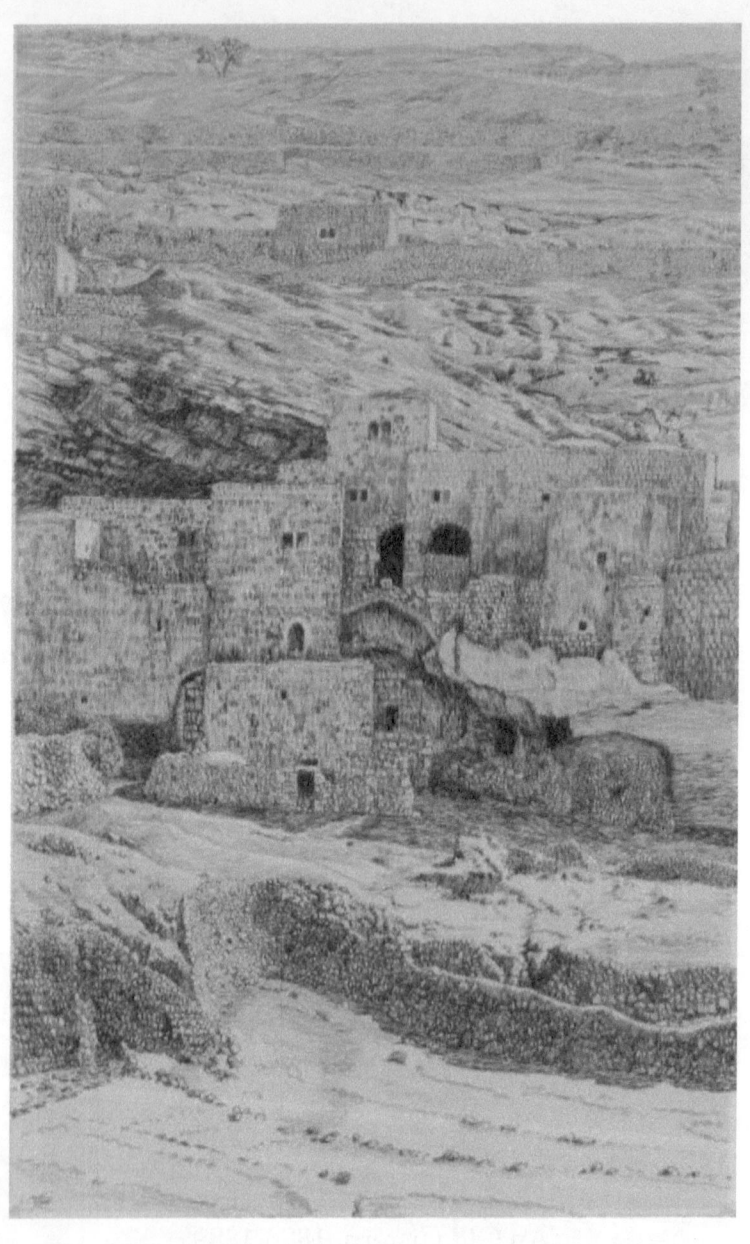

A Corner of the Village of Siloam, 1886-1889
Ink

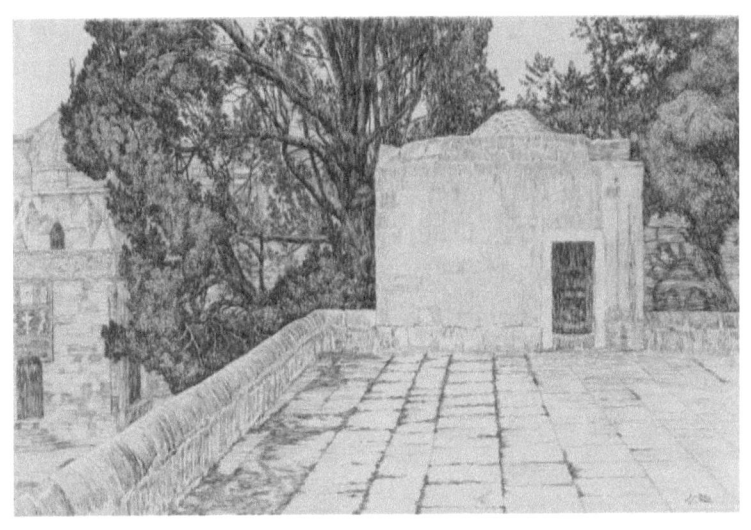

A Corner of the Haram, 1886-1889, Ink

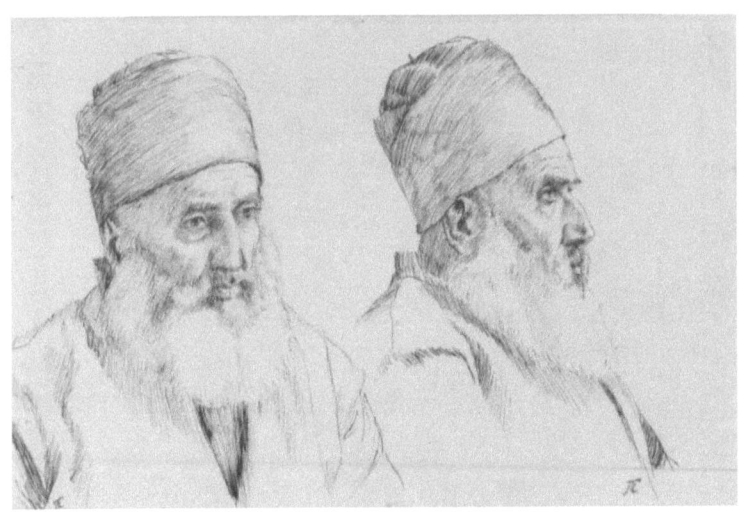

An Armenian, 1886-1889
Ink

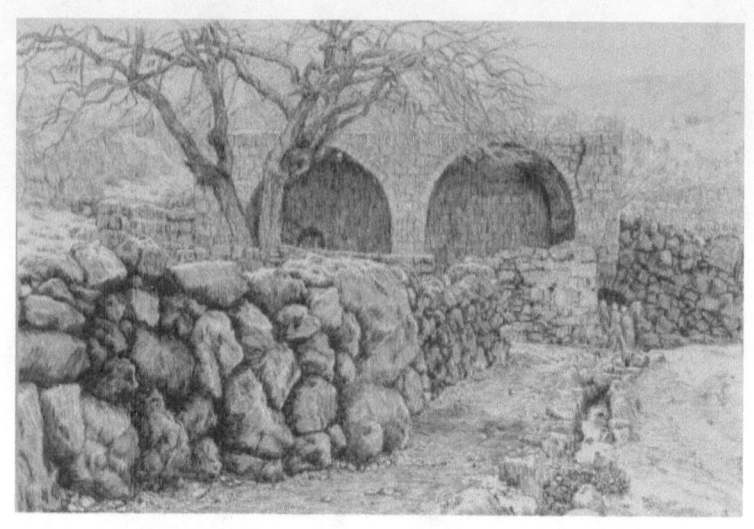

Fountain of the Virgin at Ain Karim, 1886-1889
Ink

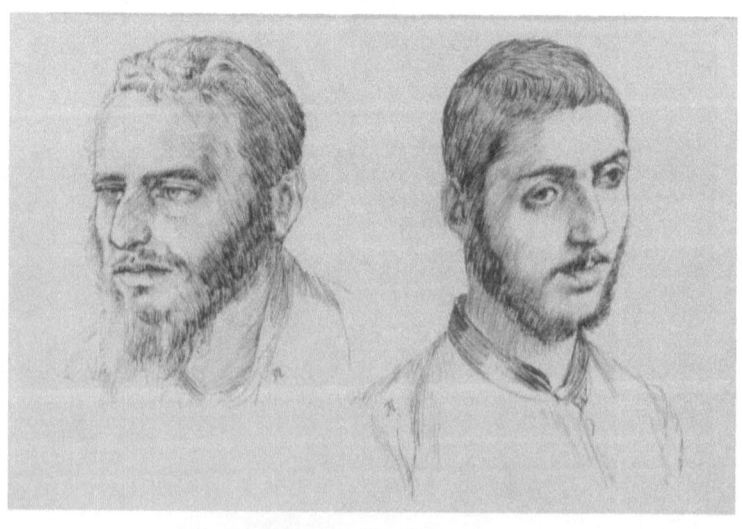

Jew and Armenian, 1886-1889
Ink

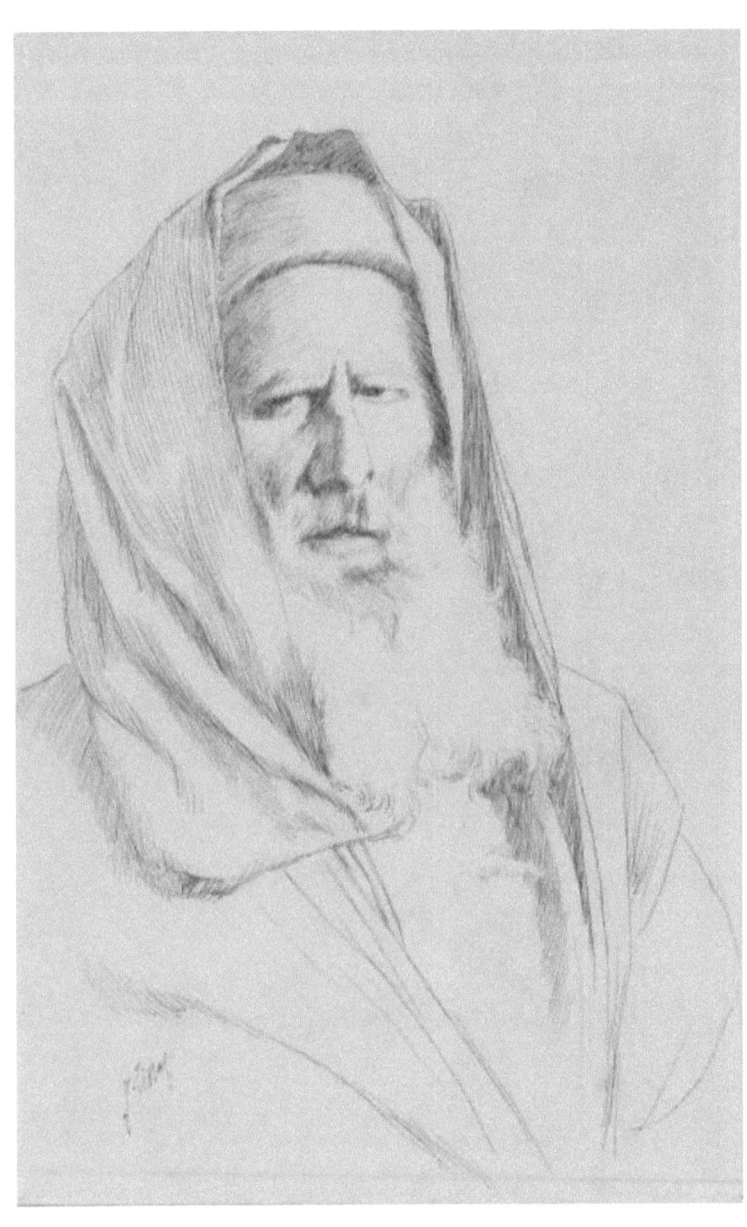

Type of Jew, 1886-1889
Ink

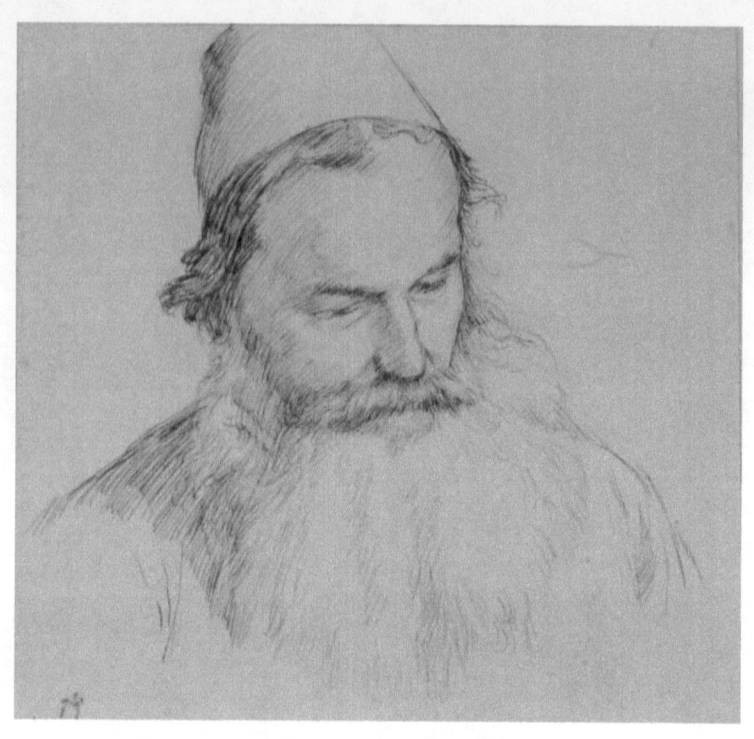

Type of Jew, 1886-1889
Ink

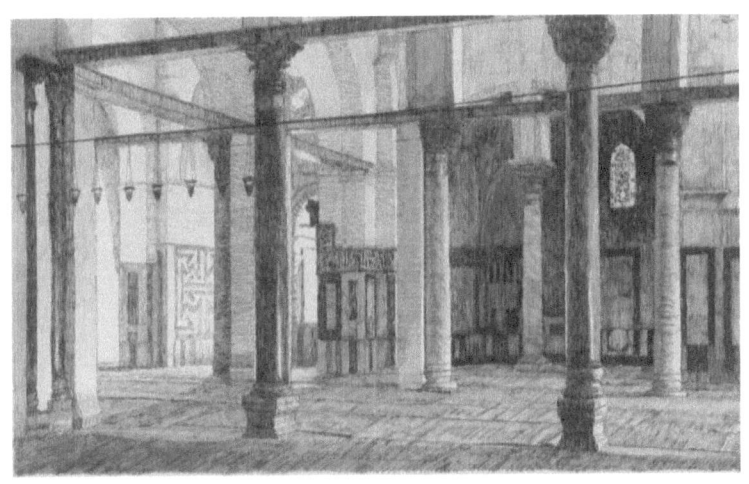

Transept of the Mosque of El Aksa, 1886-1889
Ink

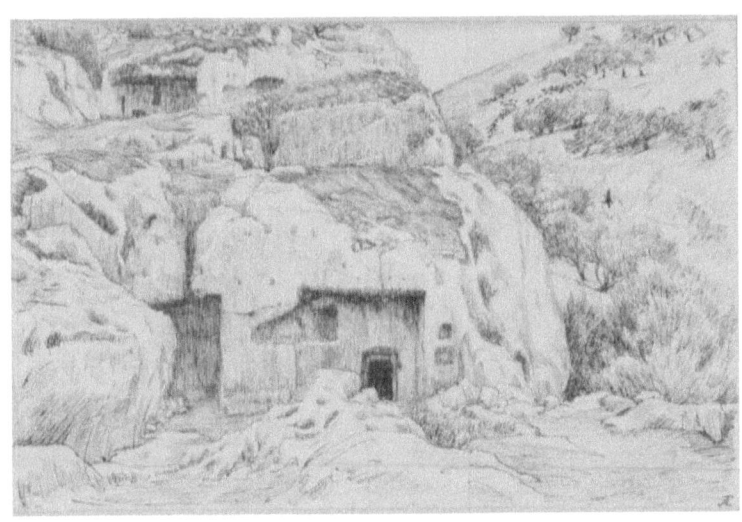

Tombs In the Valley of Hinnom, 1886-1889
Ink

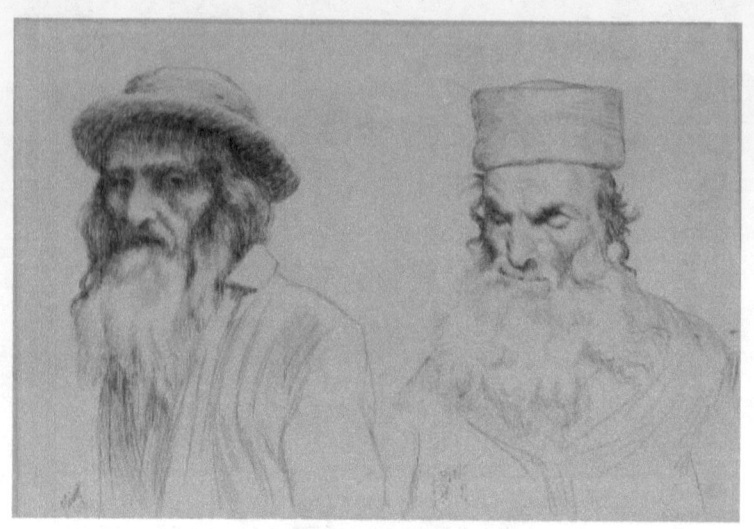

Type of Jew, 1886-1889
Ink

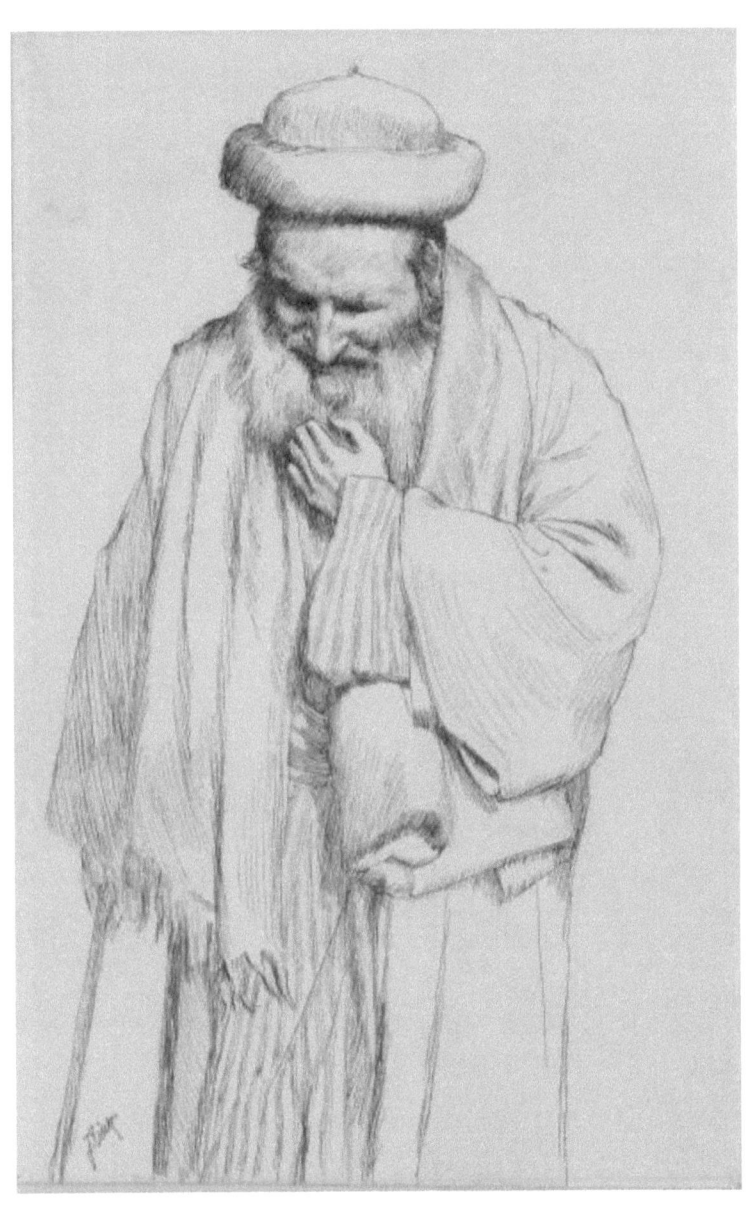

Type of Jew, 1886-1889
Ink

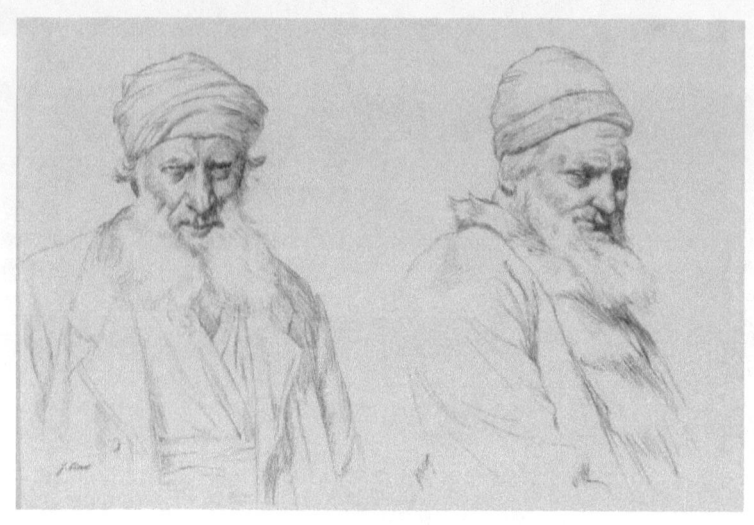

Type of Jew, 1886-1889
Ink

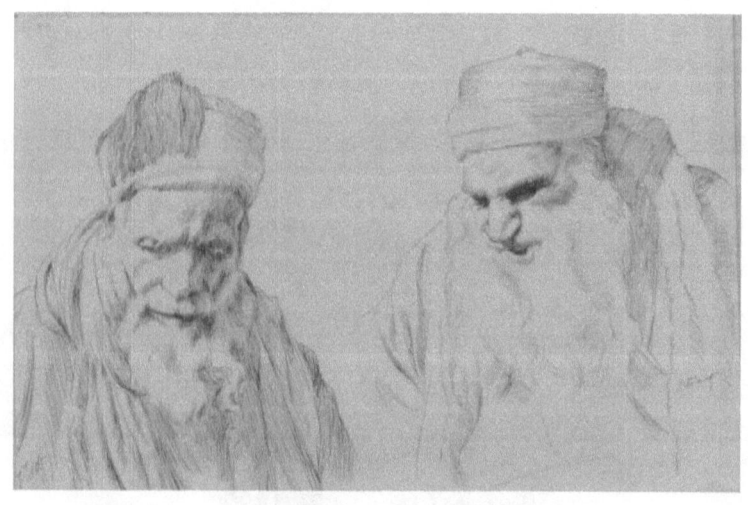

Type of Jew, 1886-1889
Ink

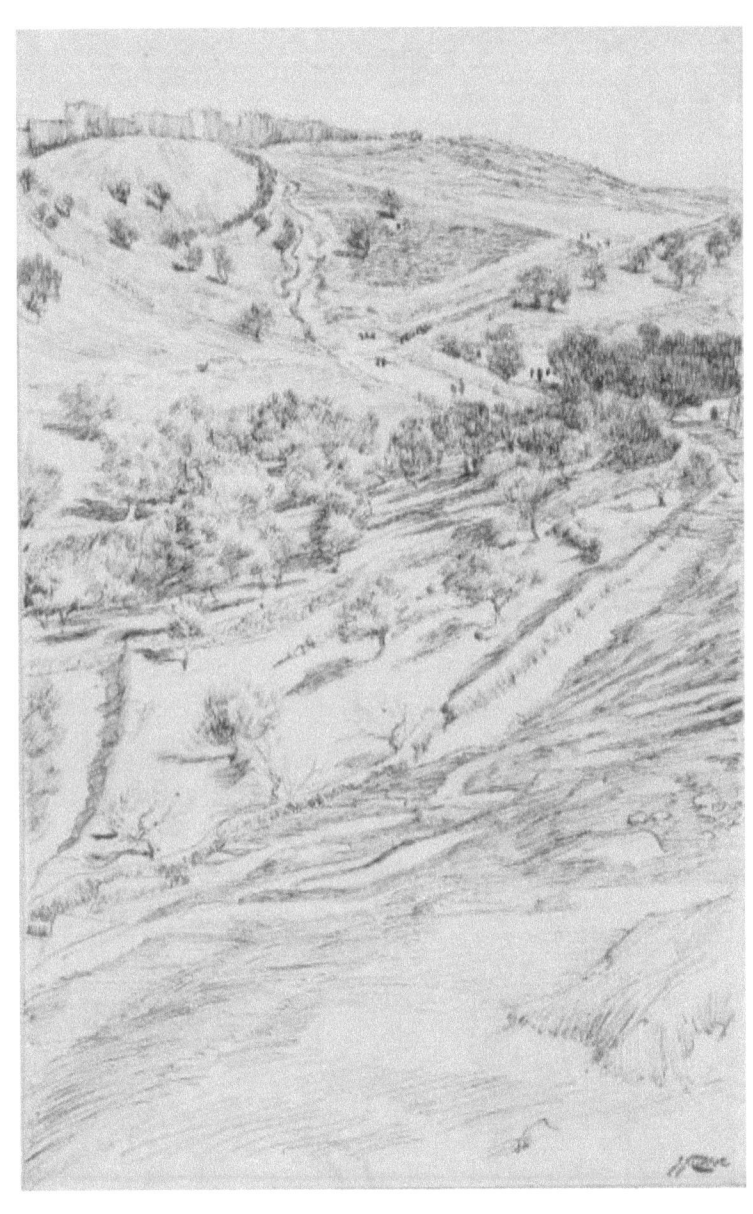

Valley of Jehoshaphat, 1886-1889
Ink

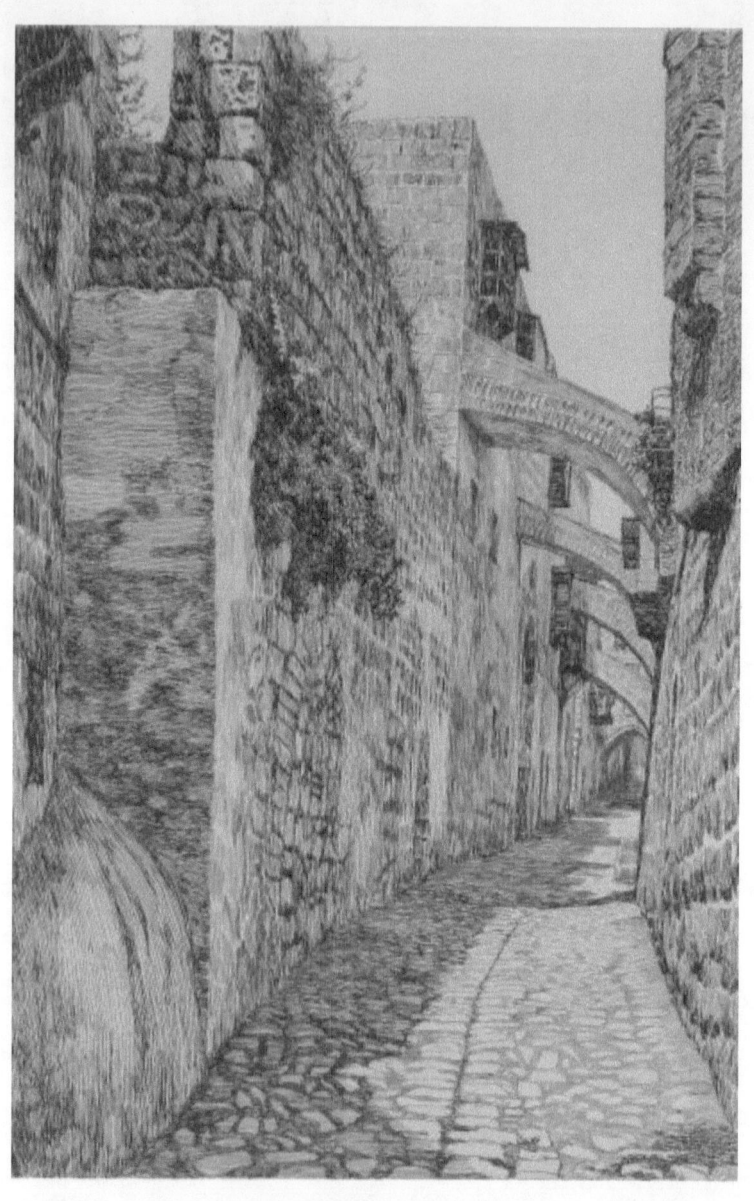

Via Dolorosa, 1886-1889
Ink

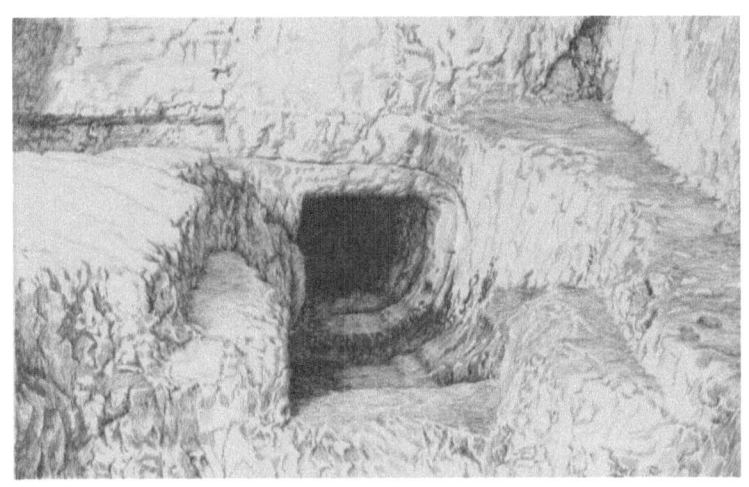

The Round Stone Seen from the Exterior, 1886-1889
Ink

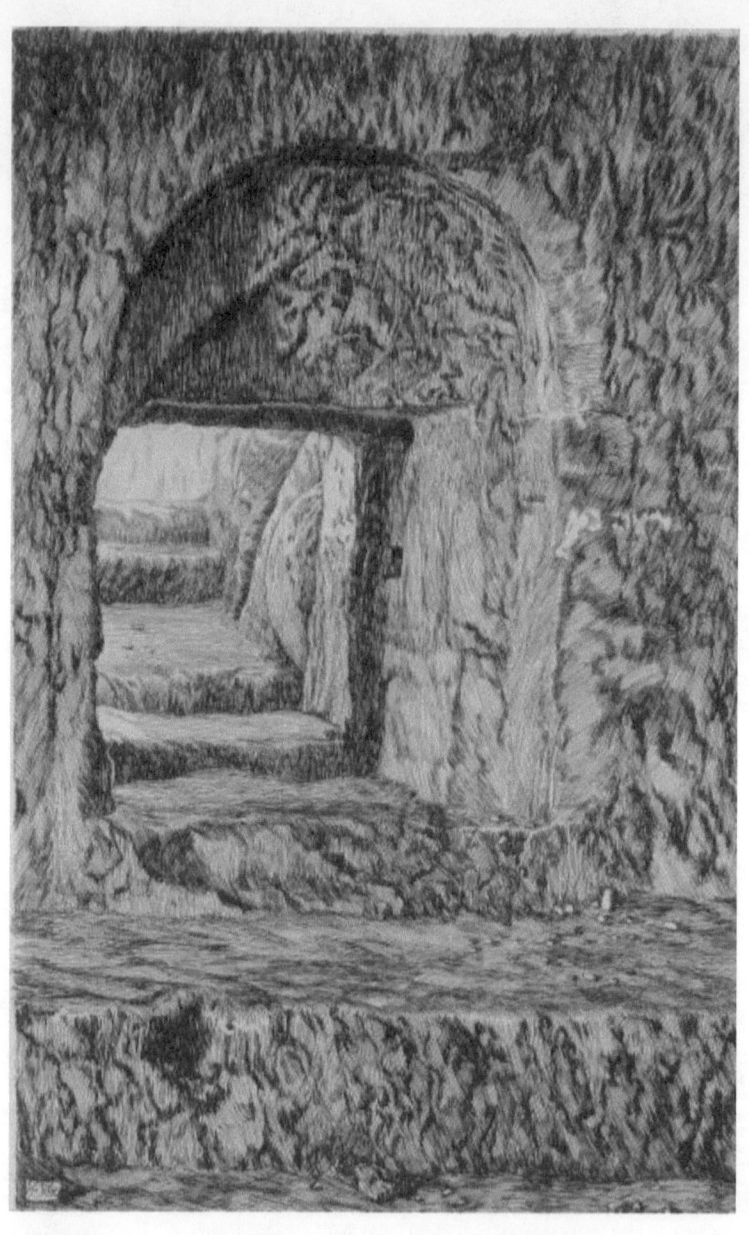

The Round Stone Seen from the Interior, 1886-1889
Ink

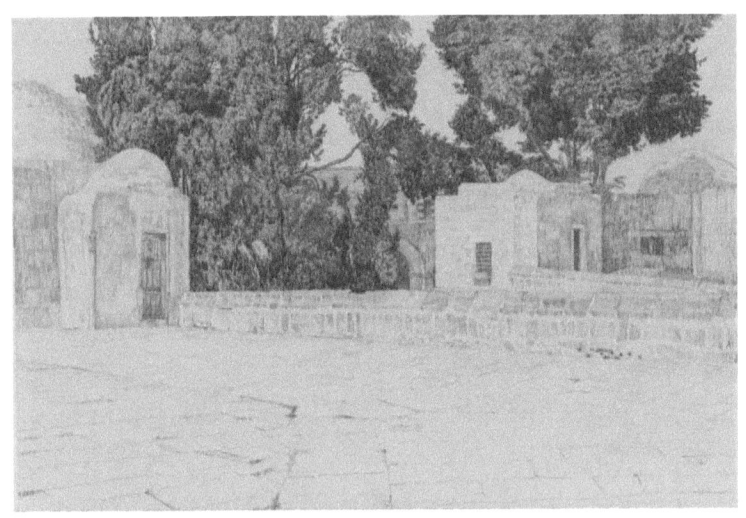

Rear of the Mosque of Omar, 1886-1889
Ink

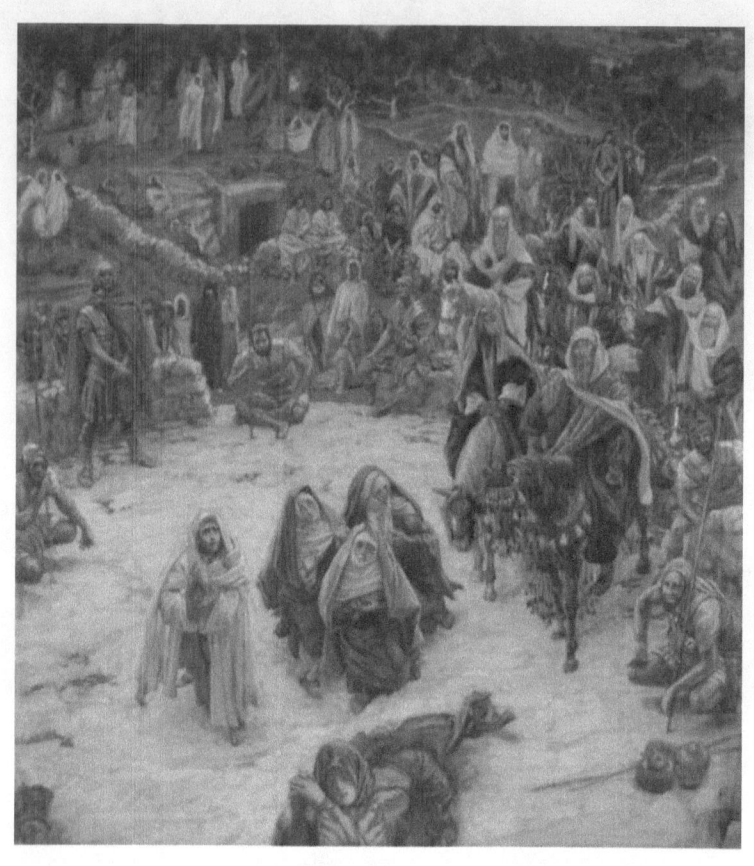

Crucifixion, seen from the Cross, 1890
Watercolor

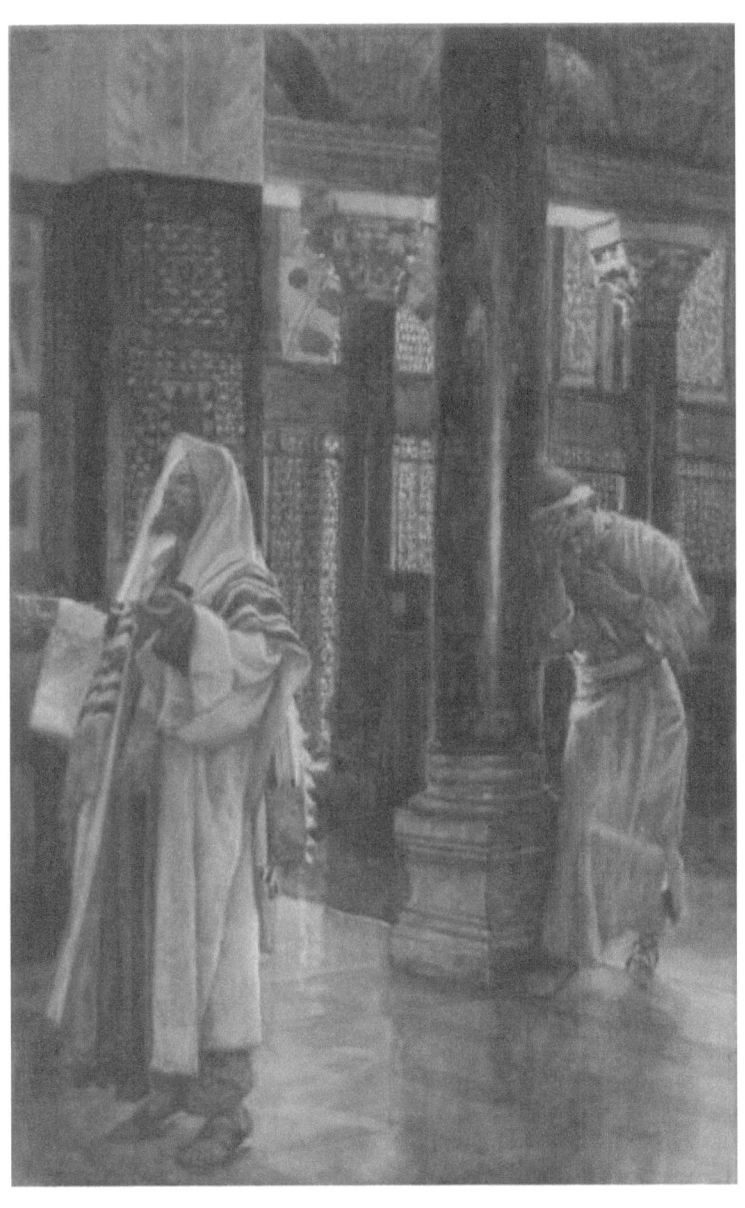

The Pharisee and the Publican, 1886-1894
Watercolor

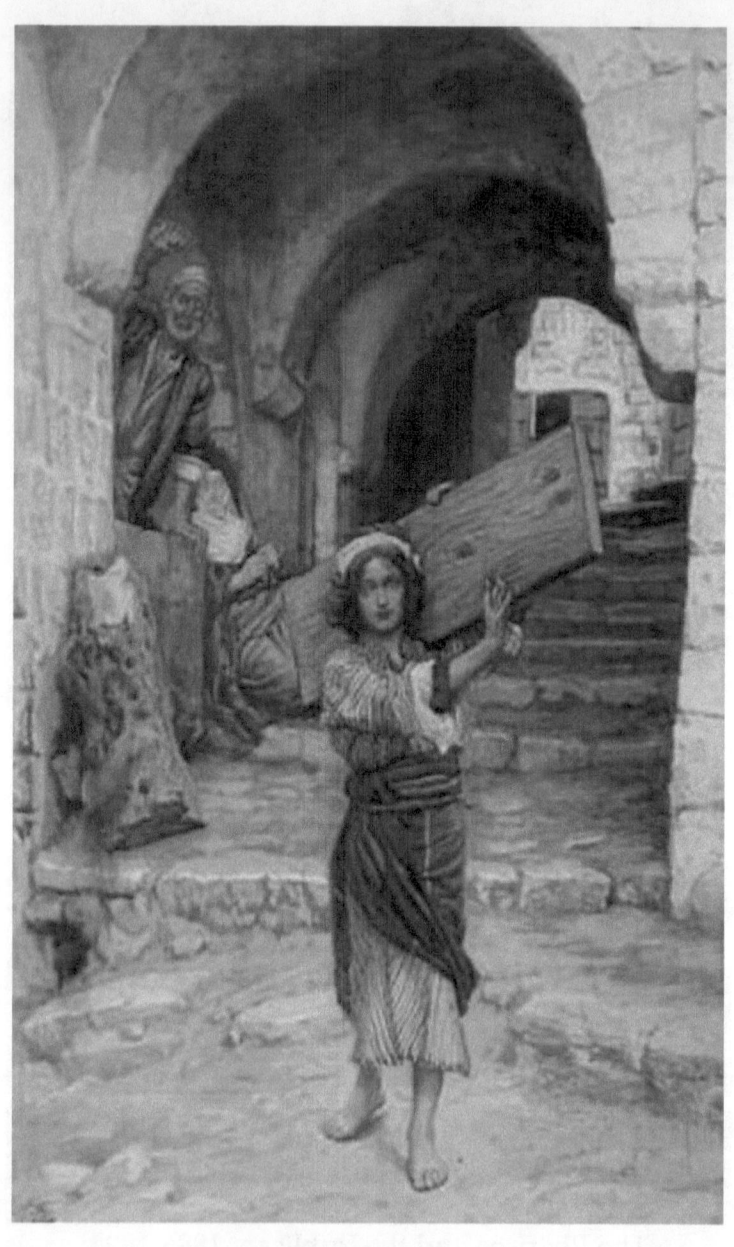

The Youth of Jesus, illustration for 'The Life of Christ', 1886-1894, Watercolor

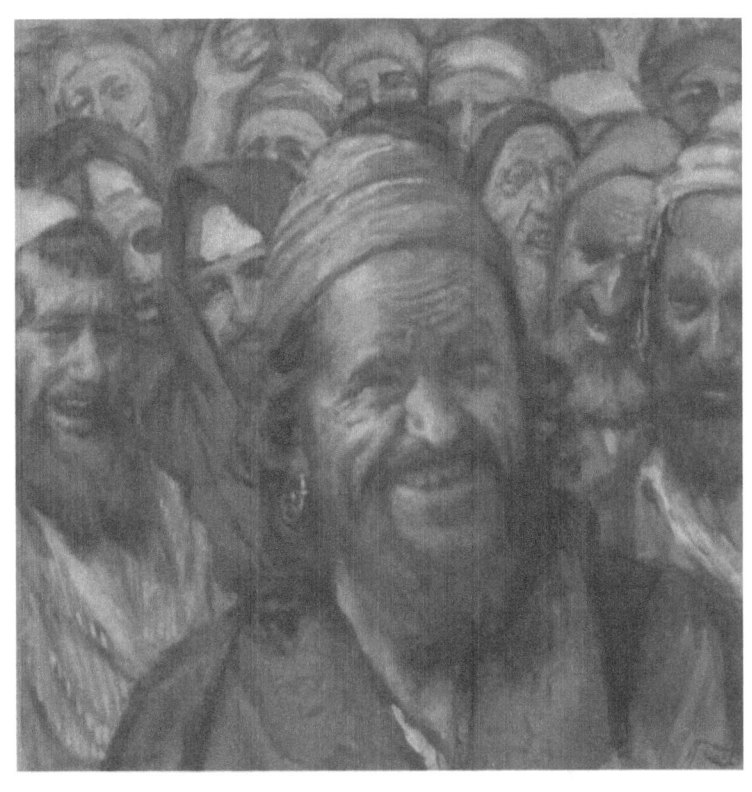

Barrabbas, illustration from 'The Life of Our Lord Jesus Christ', 1886-1894
Watercolor

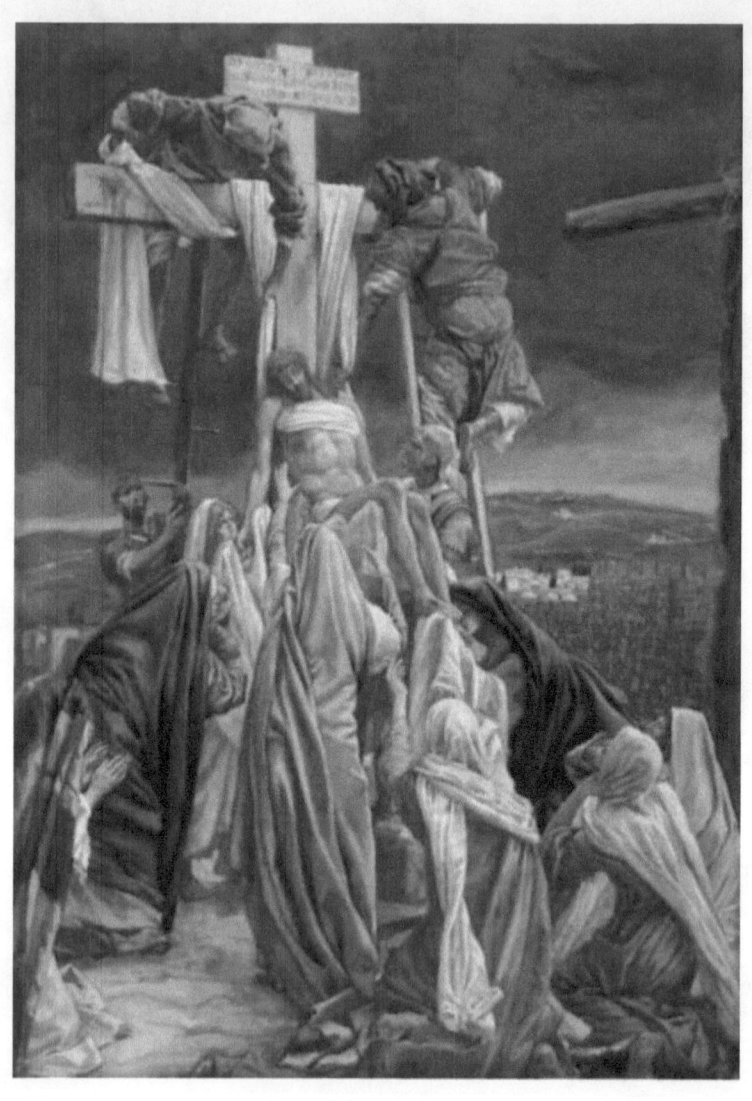

The Descent from the Cross, illustration for 'The Life of
Christ', 1884-1896
Watercolor

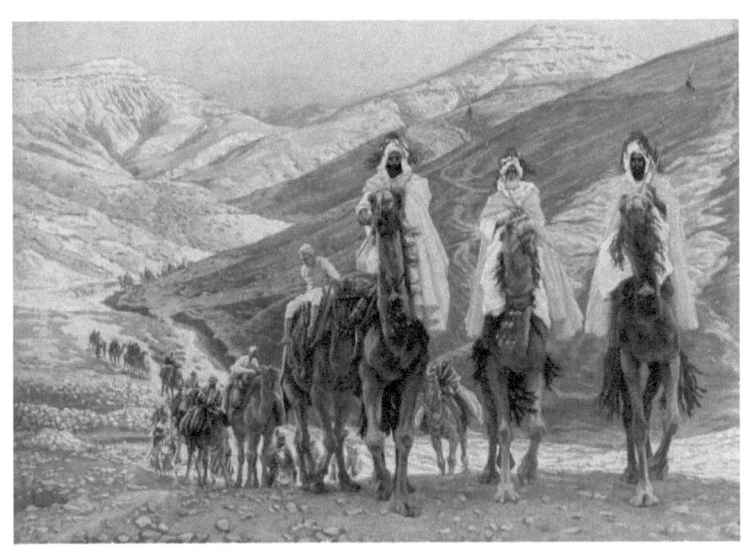

Journey of the Magi
1894, oil on canvas

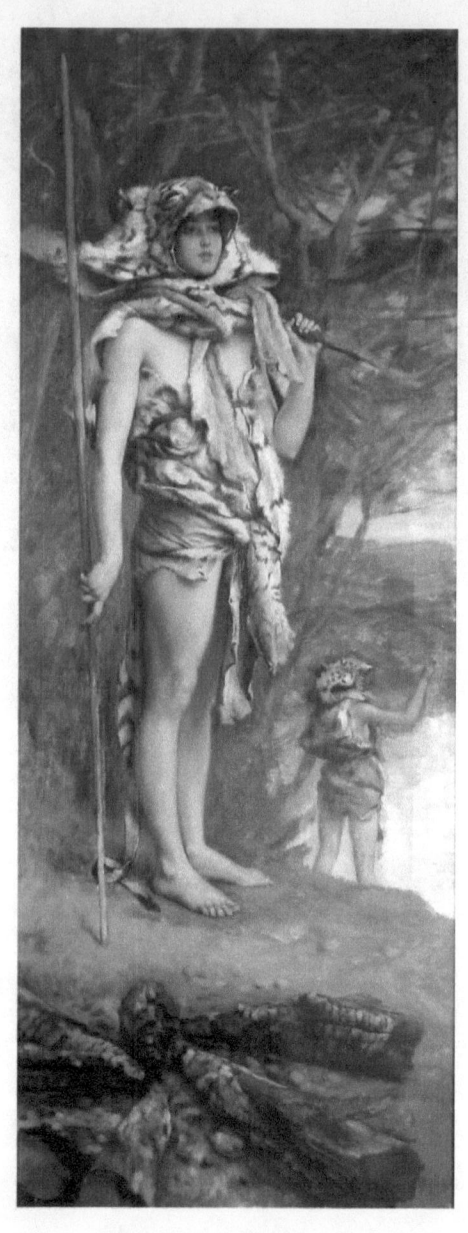

Prehistoric Women
1895, oil on canvas

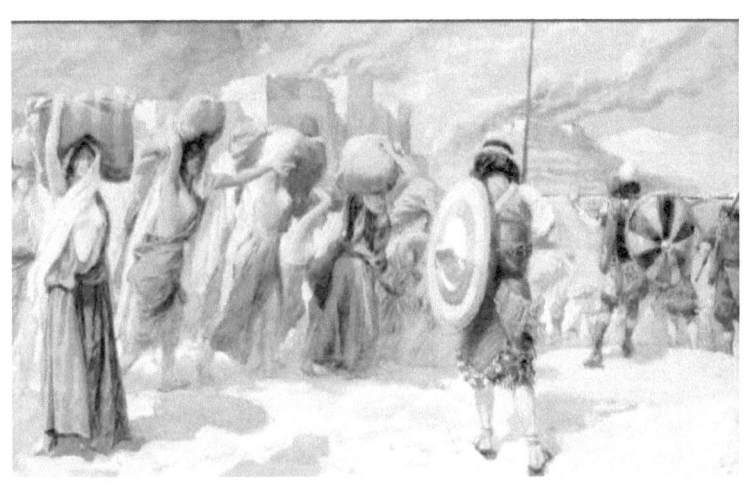

The Women of Midian Led Captive by the Hebrews,
1896-1900
Watercolor

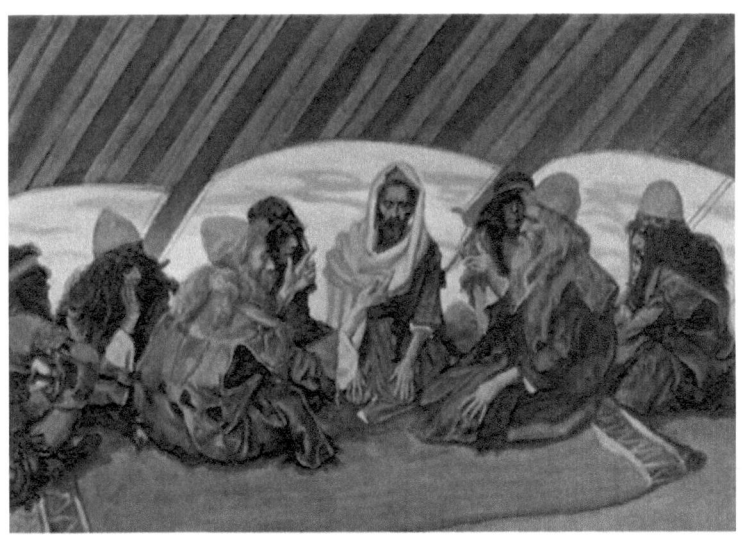

Jethro and Moses, as in Exodus 18, 1896-1900
Watercolor

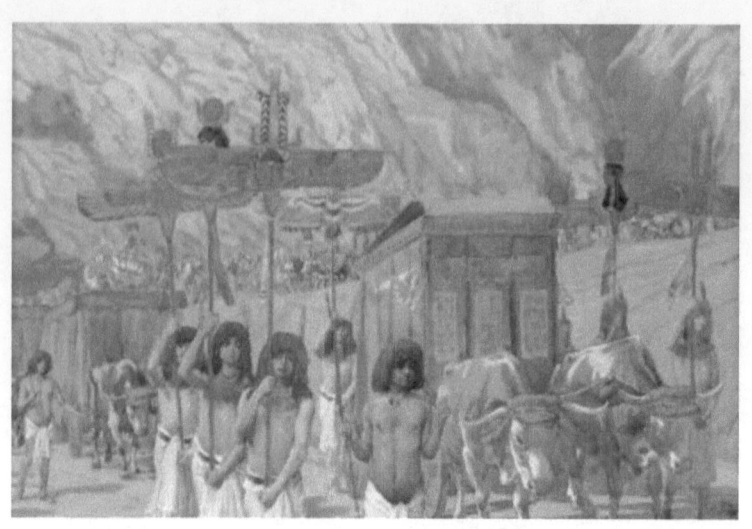

Jacob's Body Is Taken to Canaan, 1902
Watercolor

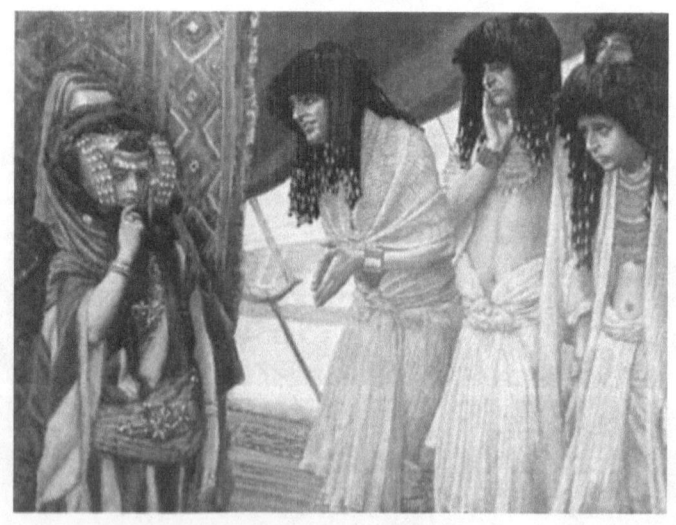

Jacob's Body Is Taken to Canaan, 1902
Watercolor

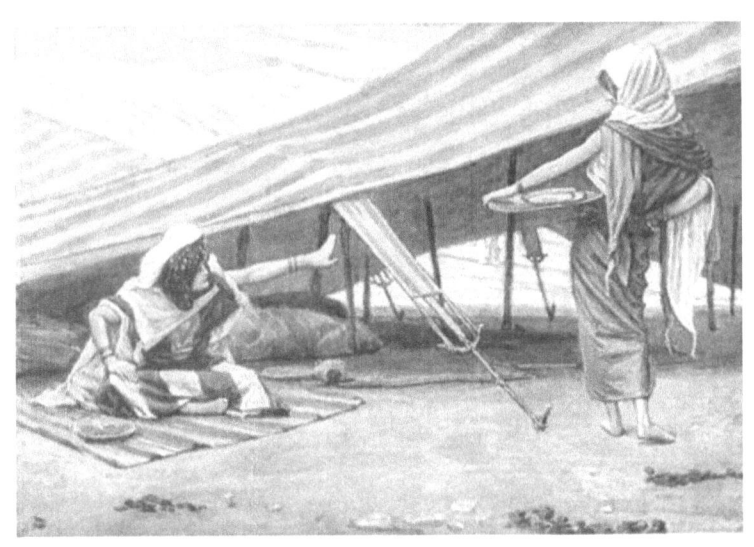

Sarai Sends Hagar Away
Watercolor

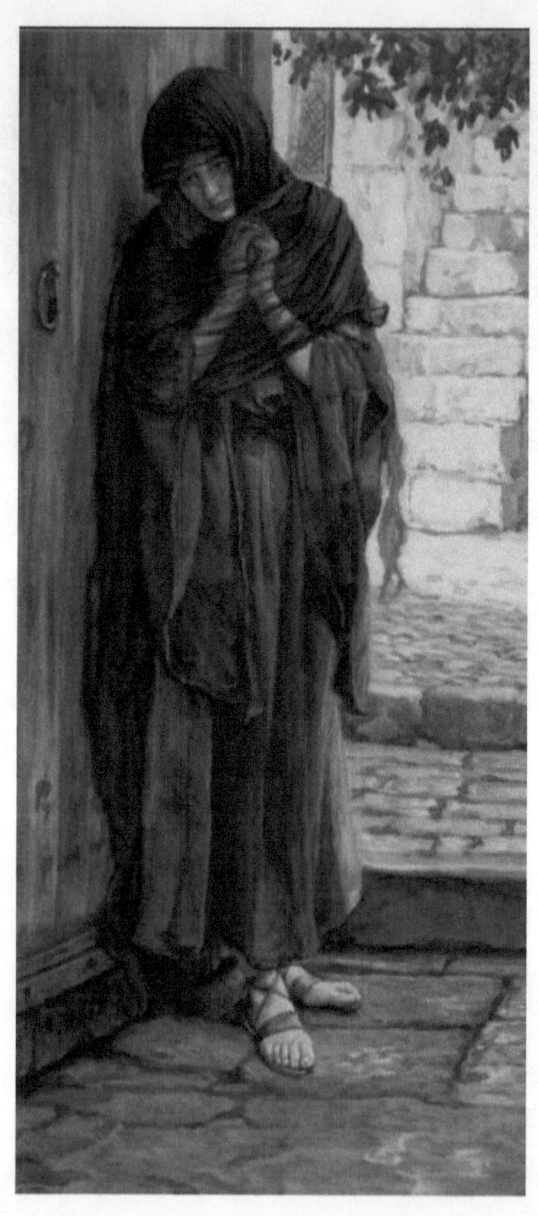

The Repentant Magdalene
Watercolor

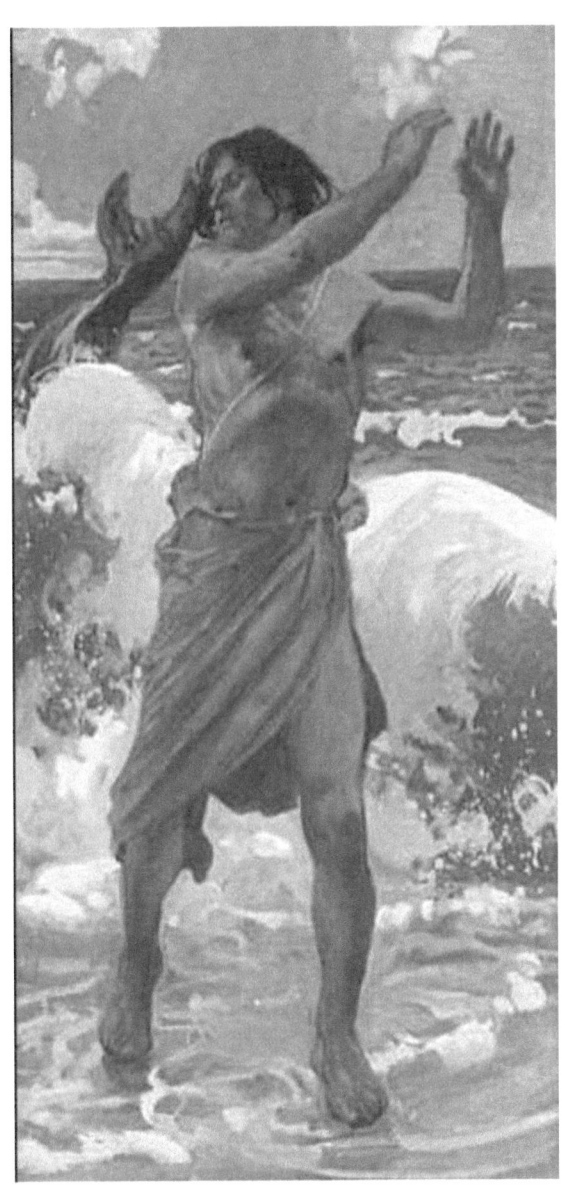

The Prophet Jonah
Watercolor

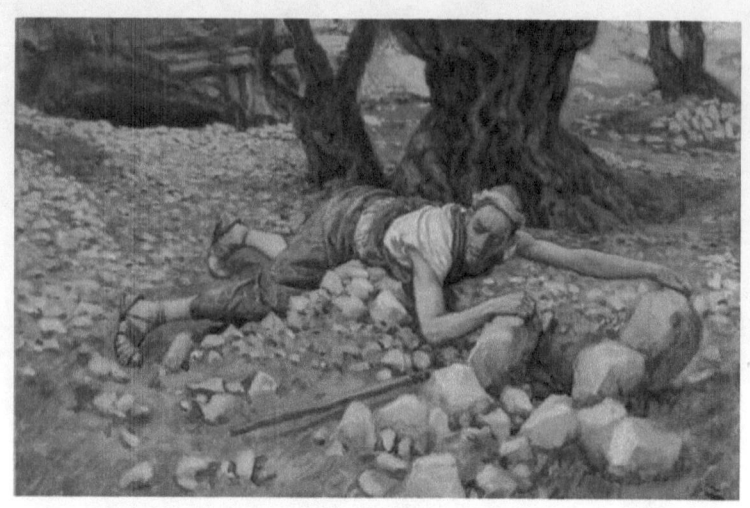

The Hidden Treasure, illustration from 'The Life of Our Lord Jesus Christ'
Watercolor

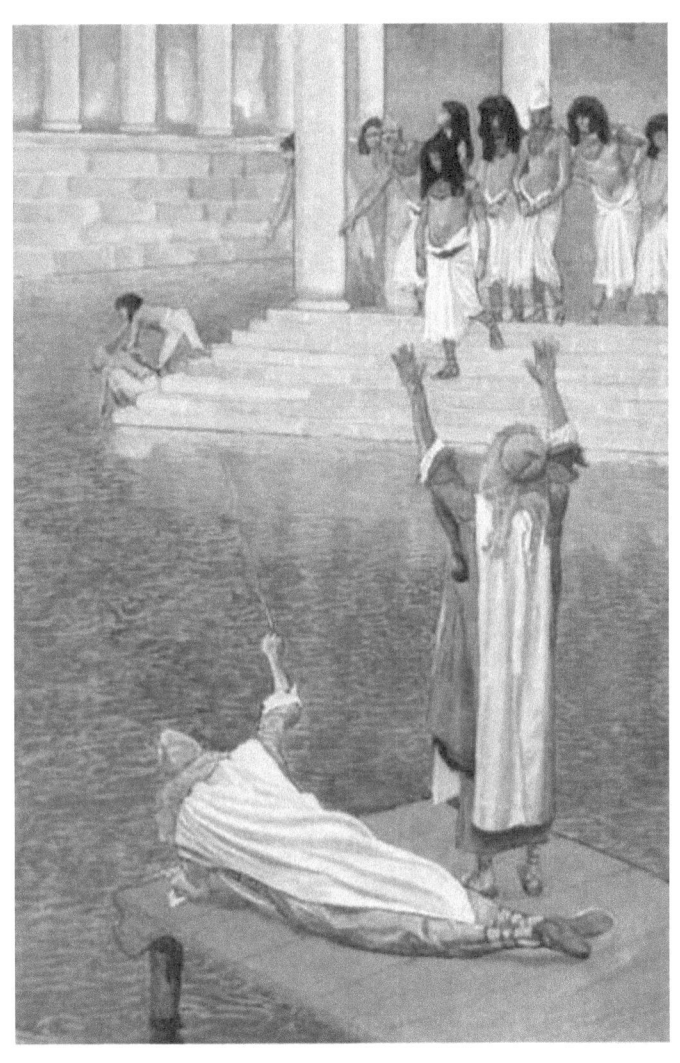

Water Is Changed into Blood
Watercolor

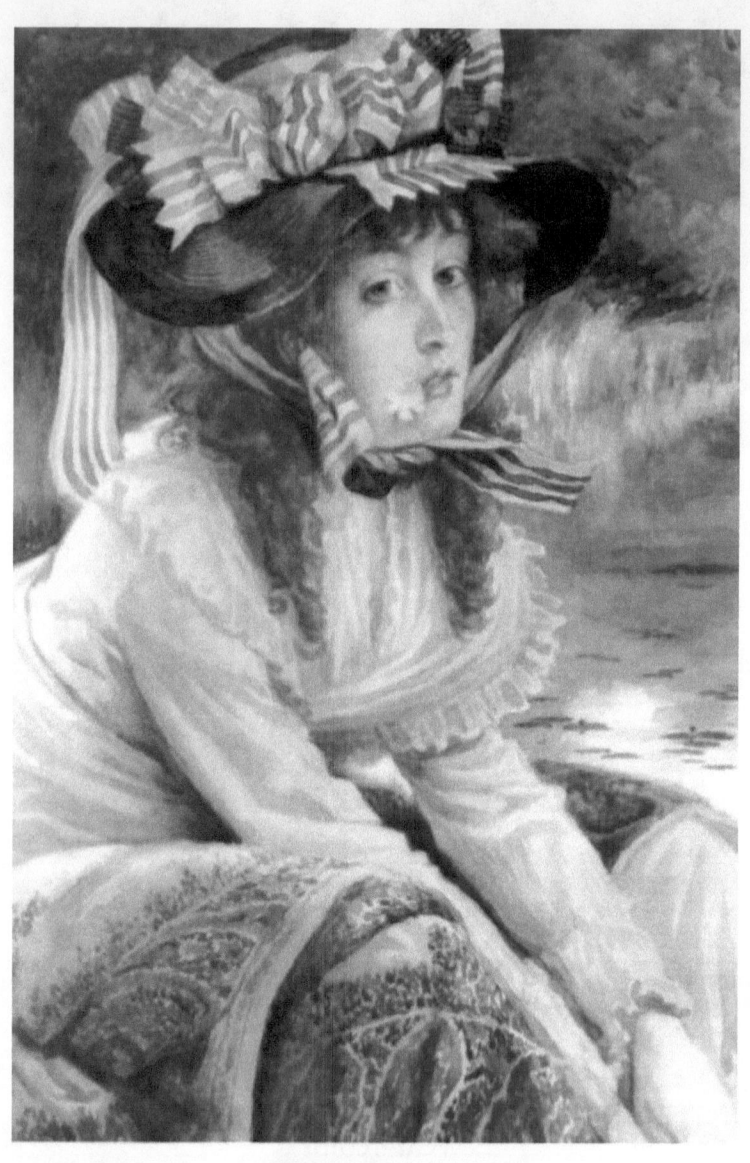

On the River
Watercolor

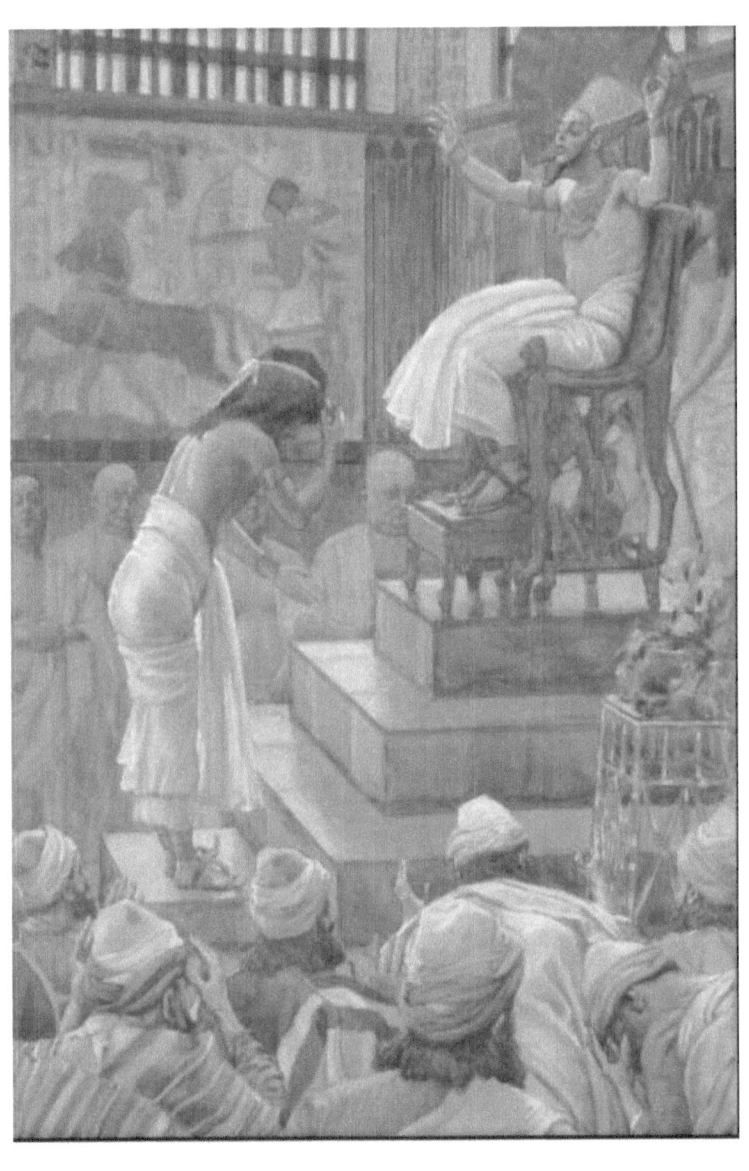

Joseph and His Brethren Welcomed by Pharaoh
Watercolor

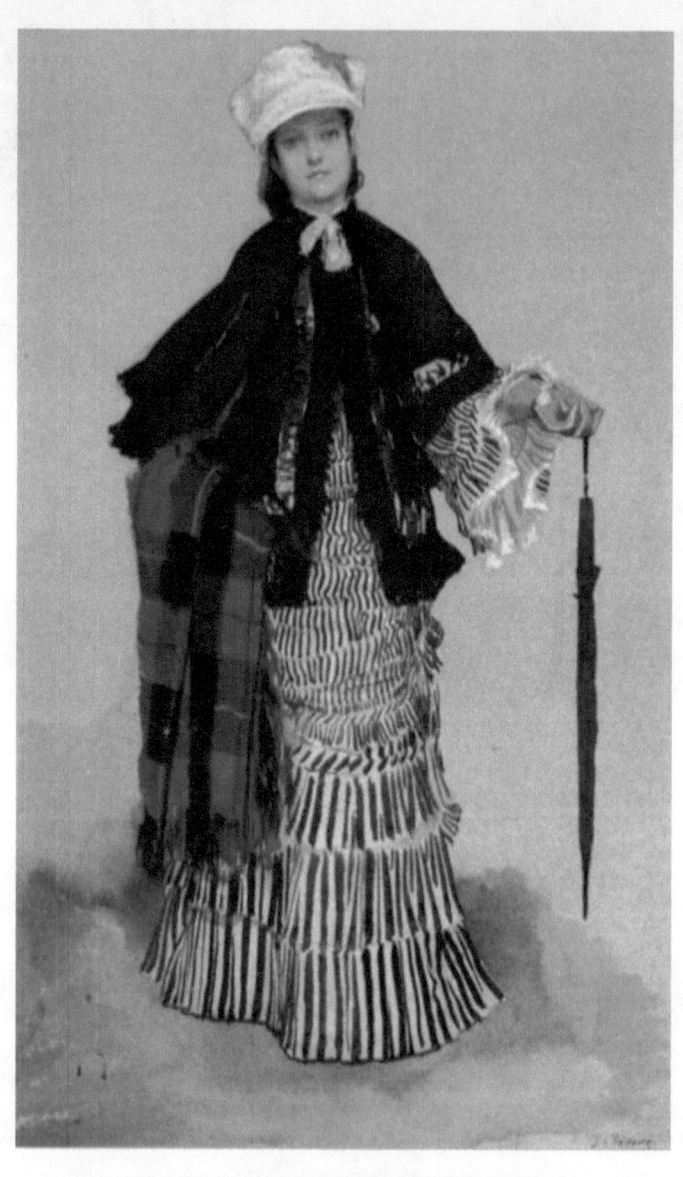

A Lady in a black and white Dress
Watercolor

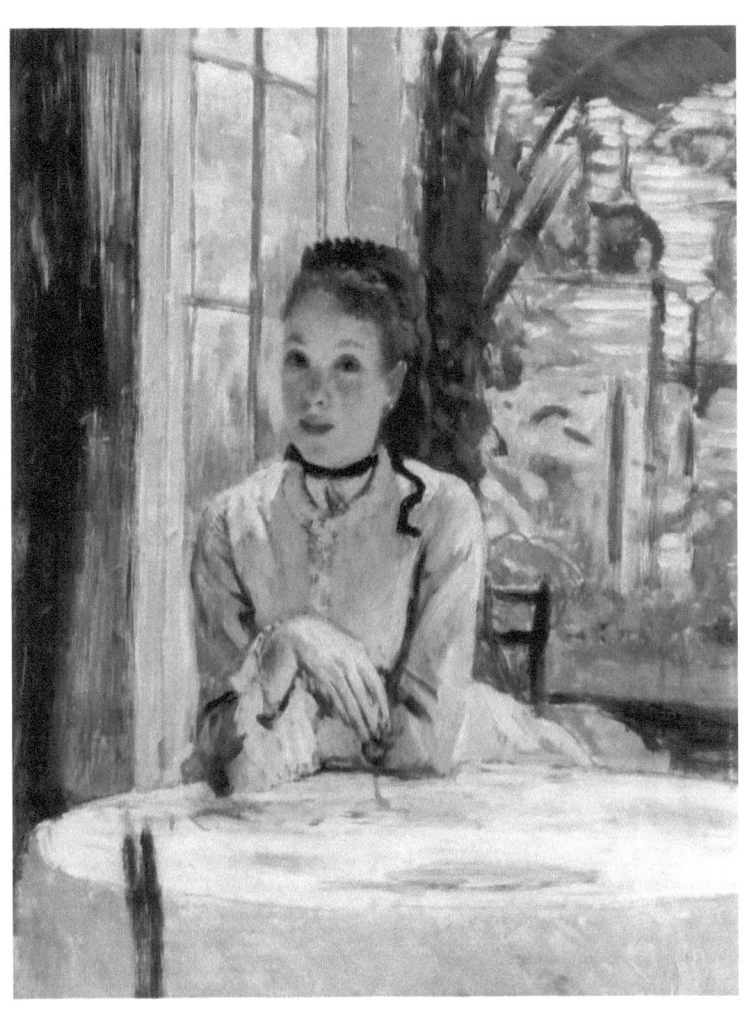

A Woman in an Elegant Interior,
N.d., oil on canvas

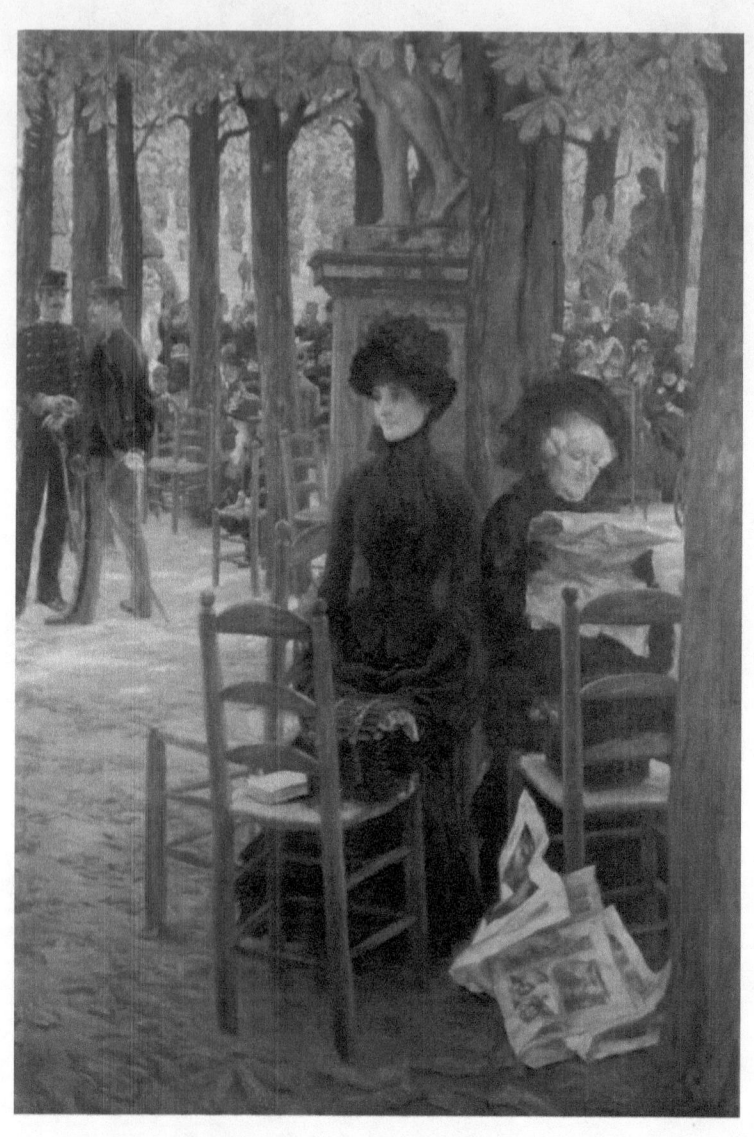

Letter with Hats
N.d., oil on canvas

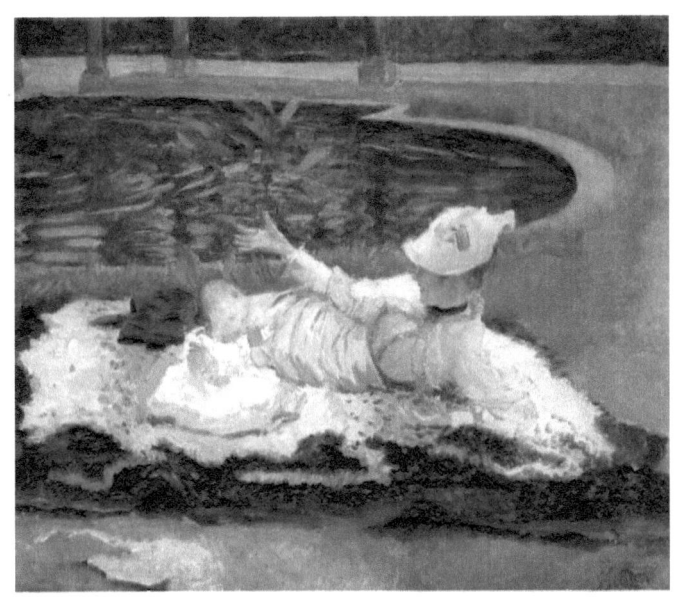

Mrs. Newton with a child by a pool
N.d., oil on canvas

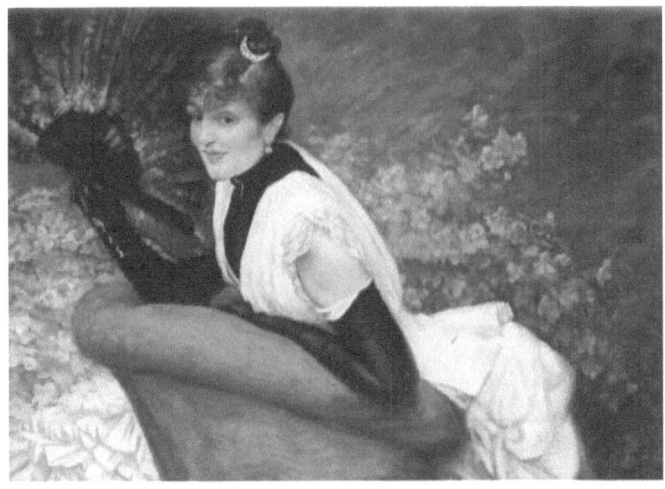

Portrait of A Lady with a Fan
N.d., oil on canvas

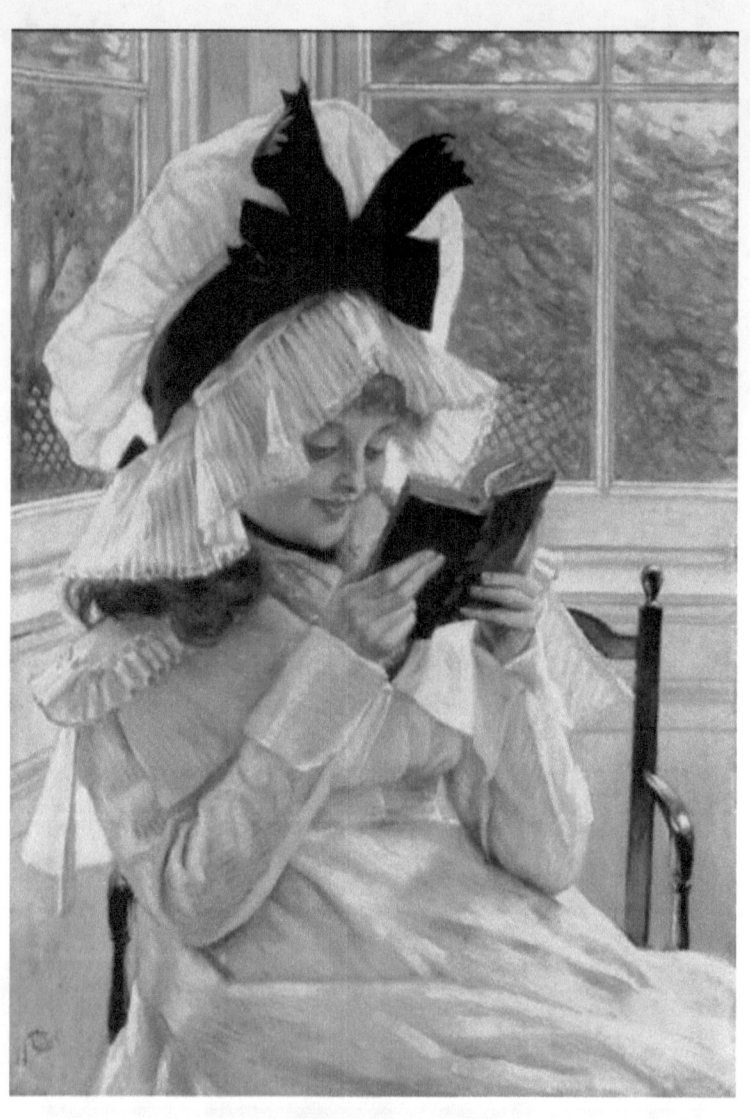

Reading a Book
N.d., oil on canvas

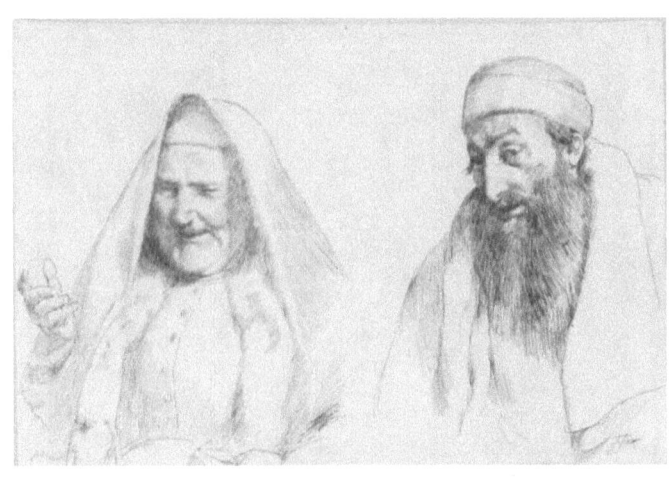

Jew and Jewess, illustration from 'The Life of Our Lord
Jesus Christ'
Ink

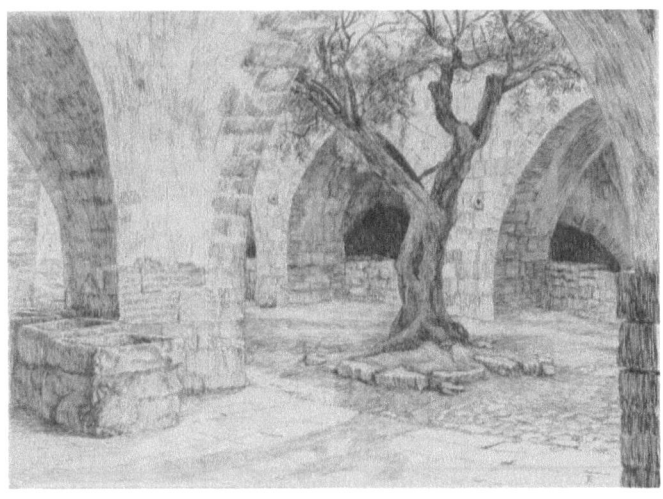

Out-building of the Armenian Convent, Jerusalem,
illustration from 'The Life of Our Lord Jesus Christ'
Ink

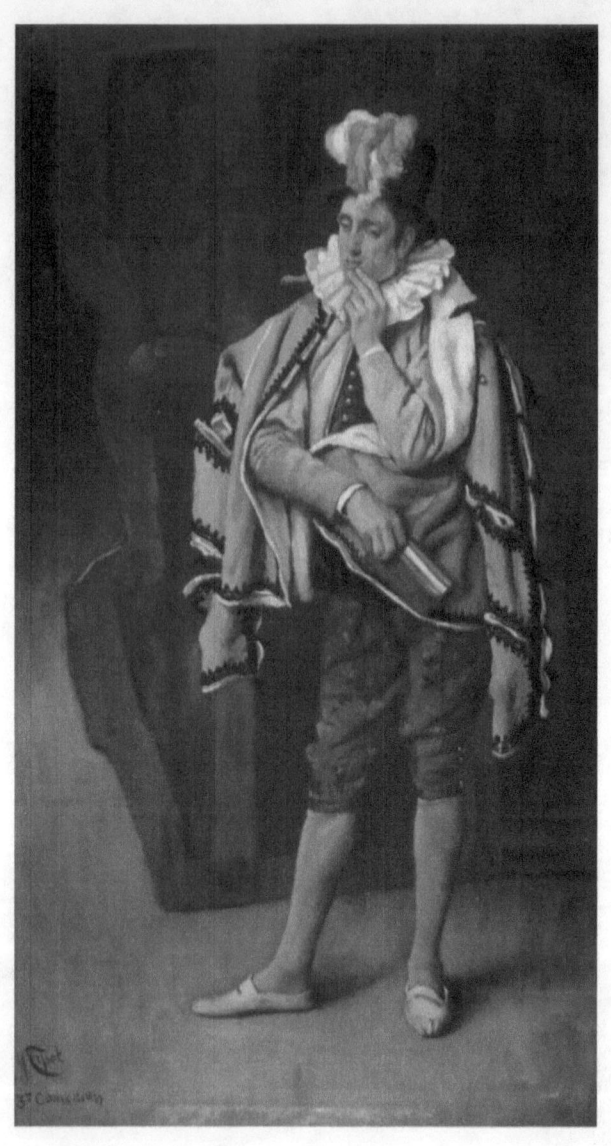

The Comedian
N.d., oil on canvas

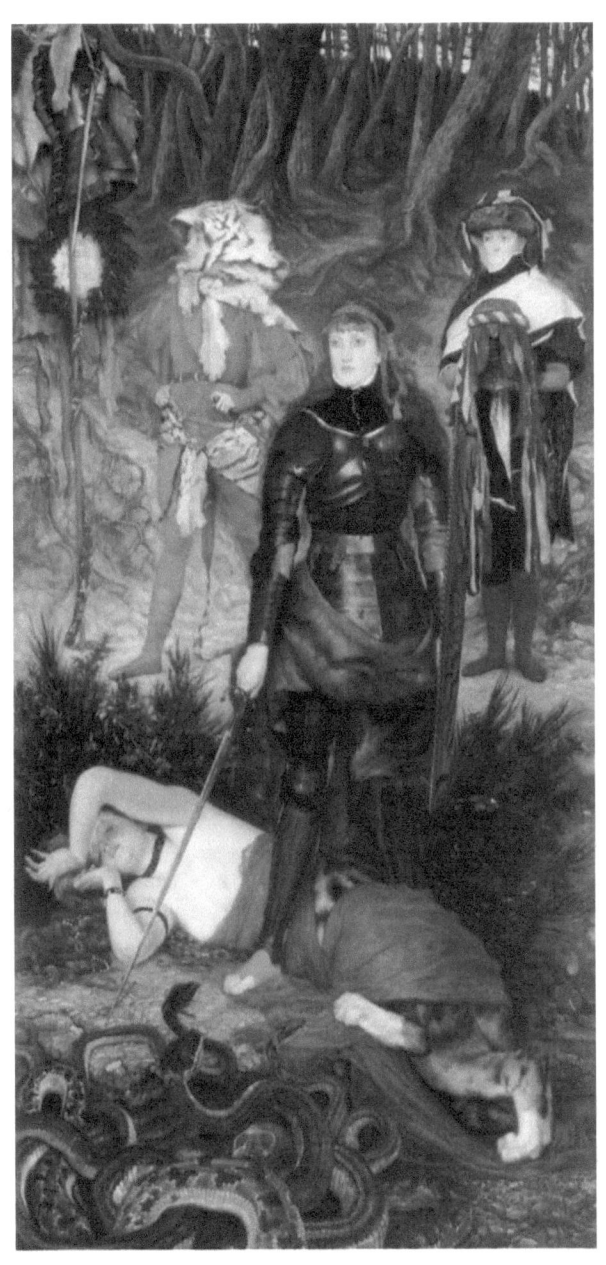

Triumph of the Will the Challenge
N.d., oil on canvas

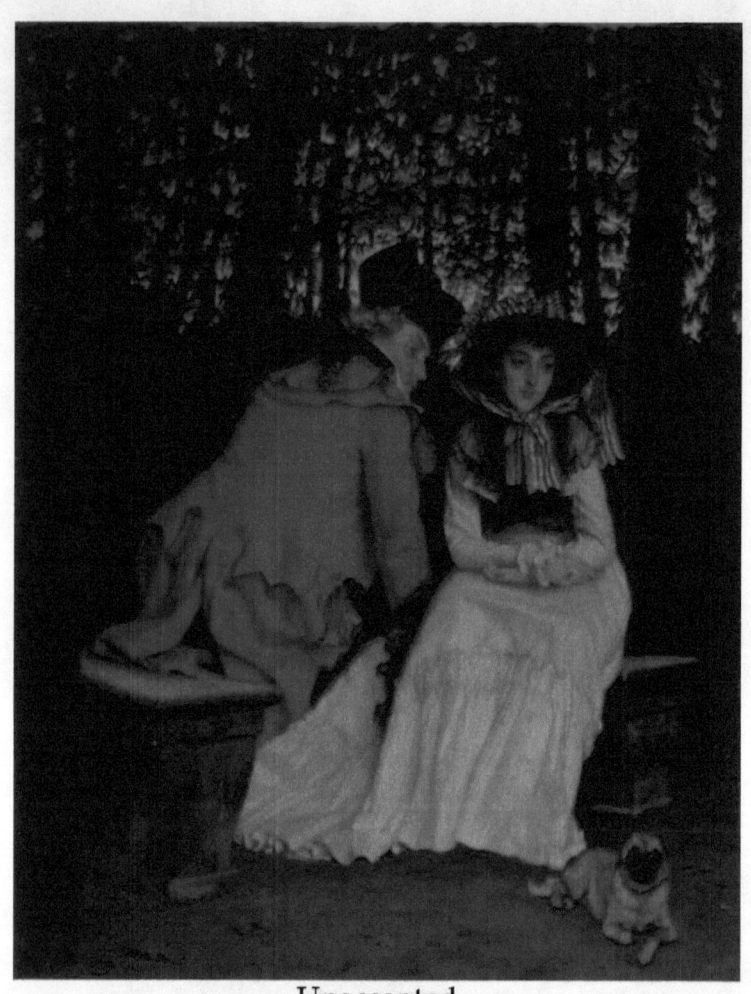

Unaccepted
N.d., oil on canvas